Hunc librum HRabani (Ita enim in apricatione germanica familiari ubique scriptum legitur) Dn laudib) Sanctæ Crucis Impressit
Joannes Anselmus in ciuitate Phorcheim, seu Phorcensi Anno dni — 1503 : Et quidē meliore adhuc methodo: Nam 5. regiones figurarū
In sequentis folij pagina prima, sunt ipsi nudi versus, quos Pr Egidius maulodice, adiutus rodice Cruciferorū parisiensiū, Hic in
margine inferiori singularum figurarū vtcumque transcripsit. Deinde sequitur Interpretatio prosaica, qualis Hic et Hic Habetur.
Sed ante sequentem Imperatoris Imaginē, est Imago Gregorij ff. 4 in throno sedentis: Ad ruius pedes — HRabanus procumbens eū
sui offert. Hanc Imaginē quatuor versus sic ly quidem cingunt: vt singulorū libros finalis hic sumatur, sicut etiā sequentis principiū
Post hanc Imaginē sequitur poema Dedicationis libri dn psalmum Bo. pont: nn ad eius successore Gregoriū 2: vt scripsit Sigebertus In
suo itinerario, sub anno dni 824. Quod œcocem statẽ Guilie dn Nangis in sua chronographia — — et alij sequuntur sunt. Quando vero
quod diximus false est.

PONTIFICEM SVMMVM SALVATOR CHRISTE TVERE

R E S V L V T E X I M I V S S I T R I T E G R E G O R I V S A L M E

T S A L V V M N O B I S P A S T O R E M I N S E C V L A S E R V A

ECCLESIE CVSTOS DOCTORQVE FIDELIS IN AVLA

Pontificem summum Saluator Christe tuere·
Et saluum nobis pastorem in secula serua·
Præsul vt eximius sit rite Gregorius almē·
Ecclesie custos, doctorque fidelis in aula·

Comendatio Papæ.

Sedis apostolicæ princeps, tu aurea Roma,
Et domus et doctor plebis, et almus amor·
Tu caput ecclesiæ es primū patriarcha per orbem,
Perorlans mœstis, et pietate potens·
Sat terræ, mundi tuæ, atque debes turbata Xpi,
Papchus perhorrens luris Ita populo·
Vestra valet cœlum, Reserans et claudere lingua,
In fœra positus claniga adherens·
Tu vocuatos ades patriæ, spes, Dortor, Honorep :
Dulcis amor cunctis, dignus amore Dei·
Tempora sunt Guiele Vitæ nunc plena periclis:
Bella mouent gentes, Gossie vbique furit·
Vnde opus est valde tua quod protectio portis
Surripiat miseros, quos triniacus odit·
Eripe sancto tuis monitis periculisque suratis
Commissum tibimet pastor ab Hoste gregem·
Vt tua laude manens, maneat et gloria semper·
Cum Xpo in cælis Regna beata tenens·
Principi apostolico Petro reiunctus in æuum,
In terris virum ruius et ipse parul·

            Offert

Offert munus Pontifici

Præsul amate deo tu Papa Gregorius oro,
Inter oues proprias me vt miserum numeres·
Gisque tui famuli probatos dicunt, et Ipsum
Altoeius domino Restituat precibus·
Qui se totum offert, parua Hæc et Dona ministrat,
Commendans tibimet seque suaque simul·
Ipse te vt alma Crucis laus nunc arreptos optet,
Principi apostolica munda, missa Petro·
Quæ Xpi ad laudem conscripta est tempore prisco,
Ludeus dum libuit carmina Dauidica·
Cedo quidem, memet per te requiescere posse·
Vitam, quam nequeo per propria merita·
Te deus actemus mundi mitissimus autoz
Tempore longæuo protegat atque regat·
Vt Valeas, digeas famulos et prospera captes
Hic : et In æternum Regna superna metas·
Te vigilem precor qui non dormitat In æuum·
Nomine atque sui Restituat meritum,
Vt vigilet cautus pastor Gregorius Domini
Sanctæ tuis ouibus: Papa beate Vale·

Hic Gregorius ff. 4 sedit annos 16. Obijtque anno
dni 844. 8 kl. februarij.

Superiora omnia frater Iacobus Du bicul, —
fere septuagenarius, se rodice Impresso
transcripsit, raliter pexsionis tuniuibus, maiora
audendi

ANGELS & SAINTS

BY ELIOT WEINBERGER

AUTHOR
19 Ways of Looking at Wang Wei (1979; 1987; 2016)
Works on Paper (1986) • *Outside Stories* (1992)
Written Reaction (1996) • *Karmic Traces* (2000) • *9/12* (2003)
What I Heard About Iraq (2005) • *The Stars* (2005)
What Happened Here: Bush Chronicles (2005) • *Muhammad* (2006)
An Elemental Thing (2007) • *Oranges & Peanuts for Sale* (2009)
Wildlife (2011) • *Two American Scenes* (with Lydia Davis, 2013)
The Wall, the City, and the World (2014) • *The Ghosts of Birds* (2016)

EDITOR/TRANSLATOR
Octavio Paz: *Eagle or Sun?* (1970; 1976) • *A Draft of Shadows* (1980)
    Selected Poems (1984) • *Collected Poems 1957–1987* (1987)
    A Tree Within (1988) • *Sunstone* (1991) • *In Light of India* (1997)
    A Tale of Two Gardens (1997) • *An Erotic Beyond: Sade* (1998)
    Figures & Figurations (2002) • *The Poems of Octavio Paz* (2012)
Homero Aridjis: *Exaltation of Light* (1981)
Jorge Luis Borges: *Seven Nights* (1984) • *Selected Non-Fictions* (1999)
Vicente Huidobro: *Altazor* (1988; 2003) • *Equatorial* (2019)
Cecilia Vicuña: *Unravelling Words and the Weaving of Water* (1992)
Xavier Villaurrutia: *Nostalgia for Death* (1992)
Bei Dao: *Unlock* (with Iona Man Cheong, 2000) • *The Rose of Time:*
    Selected Poems (2010)

EDITOR
Montemora (1975–1982)
Una antología de la poesía norteamericana desde 1950 (1992)
American Poetry Since 1950: Innovators & Outsiders (1993)
Sulfur 33: Into the Past (1993)
The New Directions Anthology of Classical Chinese Poetry (2003)
World Beat: International Poetry Now from New Directions (2006)
Elsewhere (2014)
Calligrams: Writings from and on China (2015–)

Eliot Weinberger

ANGELS & SAINTS

With a guide to the illustrations
by Mary Wellesley

CHRISTINE BURGIN / NEW DIRECTIONS

for NS, AD & H, and S

A Note on the Text: The extracts are adapted from the following translations:
John Climacus (Colm Luibheid and Norman Russell), Aelred of Rievaulx (Eric
Colledge), Mechthild of Magdeburg (Frank Tobin), Hadewijch (Mother Columba
Hart, O.S.B.), and Angela of Foligno (Paul Lachance, O.F.M.).

Image Credits: Pages 1, 2, and 88: Bibliothèque Nationale de France;
pages 10, 33, 59, 68, 99, 109, 117, 124, 139, and 148: The Master and Fellows of
Trinity College, Cambridge;
page 17: Bayerische Staatsbibliothek, München, Clm 8201, fol. 94;
pages 24, 40, 49, and 79: Burgerbibliothek, Bern;
page 152: Bibliothèques d'Amiens Métropole

Manufactured in China
New Directions Books are printed on acid-free paper
First published as a Christine Burgin / New Directions clothbound book in 2020
Design by Leslie Miller
Color production and cover design by Jason Burch

Library of Congress Cataloging-in-Publication Data
Names: Weinberger, Eliot, author.
Title: Angels & saints / Eliot Weinberger; with a guide to the illustrations
by Mary Wellesley
Other titles: Angels and saints
Description: New York : Christine Burgin/New Directions Publishing, 2020
Identifiers: LCCN 2019045191 | ISBN 9780811229869 (cloth) | ISBN
9780811229876 (ebook)
Subjects: LCSH: Angels. | Christian saints.
Classification: LCC BT966.3 .W38 2020 | DDC 235—dc23
LC record available at https://lccn.loc.gov/2019045191

2 4 6 8 9 7 5 3 1

New Directions Books are published for James Laughlin
by New Directions Publishing Corporation
80 Eighth Avenue, New York 10011

Christine Burgin Books are published by
Christine Burgin, 245 West 18th Street, New York 10011

Preceding images and all images to follow:
from Hrabanus Maurus (c. 780–856 CE) *In honorem sanctae crucis.*

CONTENTS

I.

ANGELS

```
OCHERUBINSERAPHIND    CAELONOMENIESUSIAM
EXALTATEIGNISNAMHI    CUESTERHAMINELUCET
CUMDIUITHACRUCISUER   ESTLAUSHAECUIAUITA
FRUCTLUCISCHRISTUE    NUNCQECSUITATUBIQE
UICITTRISTIATUNCRE    FIANTCELEBRANDOHIC
QIESTSERAPHINCAROR    TAHACLAUESUPERHUM
OCELESTIAMONSTRAMU    ASUNAMCONCLAMATAM
UNUMESTPENNARUMARA    RAEFIRMANTQUOQUOTO
SACRATUMATQUEDECUS    BONAQUAETRIBUITREX
EDUNTQAESITUIRTUSA    ECUMCONUSSITINIQA
CONSULTINHACCRISTUS   GAUITCALCEPOTENTES
ENPASSUSCUNCTOSQEF    USICLAUSTRACELUDRI
ETDISTRICTARUPITEX    TDEDITIPSABENIGNUS
ETUETERESACIUSTERS    REGNASABAOTHINARCE
QISSTETERATADAMSON    TNUMENHUICRIFERRE
QUAEPROBANTUIRT       CARCEREIUSSABEATUM
AUXILIAINTENEBRISI    IXUMINSTIPITEREQEM
INCRUCEFACTOREMCON

UEXILLUMFRAMEASORS    ELLINSIGNEDECORUM
PROTERITHOCHOSTESA    MACONFRINGITINIQA
SUBLEUATATQUESUOSU    RTUTISPRAEMIADONAT
NAMHIHCERULIGHSS      ITOQUETELATERENT
STAITCHERUBINHAESS    RAGASSISUNTARCAEQ
HCMICHAELABBARADANT   IGNORITEETSATISORA
SANCTARASAPIUNTUN     QUOQESACRAOPEFIUNT
UNCTATHRIUMPHAQCO     ATHERCULACONDUNT
LAETAQEDISTENSISDU    UNTHAECFACTABEANDO
INALISSENSUMTRADUN    ALMAALTAQUEPANDUNT
PENNISOSQUESUUMSER    FIMUTIAPROPETEMPUS
QUOCARNALISEATLUXU    DICANTUITIAQUEHINC
TENSACBRACHIASALU     NTISHICOFFICIODANT
HISQTRAHIATQUEHICE    SOQIUDICIOIPSEHINC
TUMDISPENSANSINTUT    MLEGETIPSAPROBANDO
QUAEIAMNOTAANTEAUC    ETCARAPROBAUITUBIQ
DECRUCENONTITUBANT    USTORUMNUNTIAUATUM
DECRUCENONFALLUNTI    TORUMSIGNANIMANTUM
```

ANGELS

1.

When armed men come to arrest Jesus, one of his followers draws a sword and cuts off the ear of a high priest's servant. Jesus tells him to put down his sword. "Do you think I cannot now pray to my Father who would presently give more than twelve legions of angels?" A Roman legion at the time had five thousand men, but Origen of Alexandria in the 3rd century revealed that a heavenly legion has 6,666 angels. Twelve such legions would have been a modest portion of what the Bible calls "heaven's army." Revelation states there are "ten thousand times ten thousand, and thousands and thousands" of angels. Hebrews merely says they are innumerable. Bernardino of Siena in the 15th century said there are more angels than stars in the sky, grains of sand on the beaches, or all corporeal things. 14th century Kabbalists, turning words into numbers, calculated that there are exactly 301,655,722, although the *Zohar* says that 600 million were created on the second day of Creation and others afterward. Marsilio Ficino in the 15th century, expanding Origen, said that there are indeed 6,666 angels per legion, and also 6,666 legions per order, and nine orders, but that the total number (which would otherwise be 399,920,004) remains incalculable. One of the largest estimates is in the apocryphal book 3 Enoch, where each of the seven archangels leads 496,000 myriads and each myriad has 10,000 angels: 34,720,000,000 angels in all. William Cross in the 18th century simply said "'tis beyond the Power of Arithmetic to compute them." Others have wondered how angels, being incorporeal, could be counted.

Surprisingly little was originally known about the angels. They are mentioned less than two hundred times in the Bible, usually only in passing. (And, in the Old Testament, when a supernatural being appears, it often may or may not be Yahweh himself.) They appear or they act, but the matter of their existence is not elucidated. Augustine of Hippo in the

4th century said it was easier to know what angels do than what they are. Thomas Aquinas in the 13th century explained that, in Genesis, Moses says nothing about the angels he met because he was "addressing an uncultured people, as yet incapable of understanding an incorporeal nature."

In the few times when they are described, the Biblical angels usually look like young men—not, as in the later iconography, as young women or androgynes or boys or babies. Only certain ones have wings. When two angels come to Sodom looking for a just man, the Sodomites find them attractive and try to seduce them. An angel with a drawn sword was invisible to Balaam, but visible to his donkey. The angel who tells Samson's previously barren mother that she will conceive a child has a "very terrible" countenance. An angel with a face like lightning and a robe white as snow rolls away the stone from Jesus' tomb to show that he has gone. (Or, in another Gospel, the people themselves roll away the stone and find inside a young man dressed in white. Or, in yet another Gospel, they find two young men.)

The Puritan Increase Mather said that angels are invisible and only demons make themselves visible. Yet in Boston in 1685 his son Cotton saw an angel with oddly Asian accessories:

> After outpourings of prayer, with the utmost fervor and fasting, there appeared an Angel, whose face shone like the noonday sun. His features were those of a man, and beardless; his head encircled by a splendid tiara; on his shoulders were wings; his garments were white and shining; his robe reached to his ankles; and about his loins was a belt not unlike the girdles of the peoples of the East.

Thirty years before, the polymath Athanasius Kircher saw another angel, reflective of his interests, in Rome:

> His head and face shone brightly, his eyes flashed like gems, his whole body was covered with an exotic robe and his folded wings were adorned with feathers of every conceivable color. His hands and feet were more beautiful than any precious stone. In his right

hand he held a globe showing the orbits of the planets, on which were little spheres made from precious stones in varied colors: a wondrous sight. In his left hand he bore a jeweled measuring rod constructed and adorned with marvelous art.

At the same time, in the English countryside, there were multiple sightings of birdlike angels. Some were of "a bluish color and about the bigness of a capon, having faces like owls." Others were "bodied like Birds, as big as Turkeys, and faces like Christians, but the sweetest creatures that ever eyes beheld." Two others simply appeared in the forms of a dove and a partridge. This had its mirror-image only slightly earlier in post-Conquest Mexico: Traditionally, the *yolia*—the life-force that inhabits the body and exits at death, somewhat similar to the Christian soul—was imagined as a bird. So when indigenous people saw the Spanish Colonial paintings of the Virgin Mary surrounded by winged, pale-faced angels, it was thought they were yellow-headed parrots.

In Ireland, the angels had no forms at all, but were blinding lights. "Woe to him," wrote a poet in the 15th century, "who, seeing the bright sun, thinks not of the brightness of angels."

John of Damascus in the 8th century said that "an angel is an ever movable intellectual substance," and in the centuries of debate about the nature of angels, it was generally believed that angels have neither biological bodies—although they do emit a heavenly fragrance—nor are they entirely incorporeal. Origen said that "it is God's attribute alone. . . to exist without any material substance and without any companionship of corporeal addition." Bernard of Clairvaux in the 12th century—who rid the church in Foigny of an infestation of flies by excommunicating them, was the author of the famous "Prayer to the Shoulder Wound of Jesus," and was Dante's last guide through the Empyrean—likewise said: "Let us assign incorporeity to God alone even as we do immortality, whose nature alone, neither for its own sake nor on account of anything else, needs the help of any corporeal organ. But it is clear that every created spirit needs corporeal substance."

Augustine resolved the dilemma by stating that angels appear "under assumed bodies."Aquinas, known as the Angelic Doctor, agreed, in his rhetorical fashion: "It is not contrary to the truth of the holy angels that through their assumed bodies they appear to be living men, although they are really not." He added: "Angels need an assumed body, not for themselves, but on our account; that by conversing familiarly with men they may give evidence of that intellectual companionship which men expect to have with them in the life to come."

This raised the question of the composition of the assumed body. Those who argue against angels assuming bodies, according to Aquinas, say that "angels do not assume bodies from the earth or water, or they could not suddenly disappear; nor again from fire, otherwise they would burn whatever things they touched; nor again from air, because air is without shape or color." They believe that angels only appear in visions, though Aquinas points out that, in the Bible, they are simultaneously visible to more than one person. Bonaventure in the 13th century, known as the Seraphic Doctor, thought that angels are a mixture of air and a conglomeration of elements. The assumed body, however, did not have the purity of the angelic essence. (As John Donne in the 17th century put it: "Then as an angel, face, and wings / Of air, not pure as it, yet pure doth wear, / So thy love may be my love's sphere.") Aquinas, however, said they are purely air: "Although air as long as it is in a state of rarefaction has neither shape nor color, yet when condensed it can both be shaped and colored as appears in the clouds. Even so the angels assume bodies of air, condensing it by the Divine power in so far as is needful for forming the assumed body." He also noted that they are completely transparent.

Since they are beings made of air, when, in the Bible, they eat and drink—as the guests of Abraham and in other instances—they are only seeming to eat and drink. Aquinas called this "figurative of spiritual eating." In the semi-apocryphal Book of Tobit, the archangel Raphael explains it more precisely to Tobias: "When I was with you, I seemed indeed to eat and to drink; but I use an invisible meat and drink." But pretending to eat and drink, or assuming a human body, is a form of deception. This was a theological conundrum: Demons of course deceive, but are angels, who are purely good, capable of deception? Some said they were deceiving for a higher good; some said, despite any Biblical evidence, that they made it clear that they were angels and not men.

Pragmatic Protestants resolved or avoided the question by declaring that the angels' assumed bodies were real bodies and that they really ate—though some claimed that what they ate was "angels' food." John Calvin in the 16th century: "I doubt not, but that God which made all the world of nothing, and which is a wonderful workmaster in fashioning his creatures, gave unto them bodies for a time, wherein they might do that office which was committed unto them. And as they did truly walk, speak, and do other duties, so I judge that they did as truly eat." John Milton in the 17th century dismissed the idea that angels do not eat as "the common gloss of theologians." The angels of *Paradise Lost* have ravishing appetites and even—though not described in detail—digestive systems.

From the beginning, the early and medieval scholars faced many quandaries. Ethereal beings presumably cannot have any physical and sensory organs. So if the proverbial "tongues of angels" do not exist, how do they speak to men and to each other, or sing their praises to God in heaven? Augustine, syntactically anticipating Gertrude Stein, declared that "God does not speak to the angels in the way that we speak to each other, or to God, or to the angels, or as the angels speak to us, or as God speaks to us through them." God and the angels speak without sound—without "noisy, spoken words"—and are heard by "inward" or "mental" ears.

Aquinas similarly said that the angels talk to each other by "interior speech," sending thoughts with their will—a kind of telepathy that can move across great distances instantaneously. The "tongues of angels" is merely a metaphor for the "power they have to make their thoughts known." However, when an angel speaks to a human, he "does not really speak through his assumed body; he only imitates speech, forming sounds in the air corresponding to human words." Just as they condense the air to become visible, they condense the air to create sounds. This explanation was generally accepted for centuries. As for the content of this imitation speech, it remained debatable whether the angels are speaking on their own, or whether God is speaking through them—in our terms, whether they are cognizant individuals or radios.

Nevertheless, they somehow produce beautiful music. Humilitas of Faenza in the 13th century, who lived attached to the church of St. Apollinaris in a windowless cell with only a small slit so she could follow the mass and receive communion, heard them: "Whenever they unfurl their wings in flight and then gather them gracefully together again, they make their ministry a sweet song. Since they are spirits endowed with the power of the most high, they make a song that no other creature is able to sing."

Their lack of sensory organs raised the question of what the angels can see or hear or experience—and what, if they could not experience anything, they could learn or know or remember, or whether they had memories at all. Aquinas countered the objections, first by noting that the angels in their appearance are seen to have sensory organs, and that

> in the works of the angels there is nothing without a purpose. But eyes, nostrils, and the other instruments of the senses, would be fashioned without a purpose in the body assumed by the angel, if he perceived nothing by their means. Consequently, the angel perceives by the assumed body.

As to how the angels perceive, he is uncharacteristically vague:

> Experience can be attributed to the angels according to the likeness of the things known, although not by likeness of the faculty knowing them. We have experience when we know single objects through the senses: the angels likewise know single objects. . . yet not through the senses. But memory can be allowed in the angels, according as Augustine puts it in the mind; although it cannot belong to them in so far as it is a part of the sensitive soul.

CRUX·ROGO·SACRA·DET·C GNAMI·HR·NUMINE·PE·ET
LAUDIBUS·UT·CLARA·CA RE·MTUA·RITE·TROPAEA
QUOMODO·TERRENIS·AB AELIS·FOEDERA·DUCAS
PACTUM·CONFIRMES·ER OET·VINCULA·RUMPAS
QUOS·ARMENA·OL·CATHOLIC MTUMARTIRUMET·OR·DO
IURE·D·OMUS·XPI·POCUI QUOS·CULMEN·IN·PLUM
COND·SCISSIMA·PLEBS LWE·ST·VOCE·REPERTA
FAUC·DA·SALUTARI·SER RUX·S·UNDAM·TNE·CUMMO
IUSI·DA·CONSTRUCTA UCIS·IXI·ROBORE·FIXA
QUAE·VERE·HUMANI·GEN SADU·ITAM·DEDI·AUIT
FIRMATAQ·COLUMNA·E ITOCTENDERE·PHILAR
ETE·VNAM·PER·SE·PARA YSLO·CURGERE·FORMAM
EGMINIS·ET·AULA·MISP UST·VLCTI·QUO·REGIS
RIS·VERVQUAE·ANQUA OXIVRE·CVRERE·ITAQE
FRIGISIN·MUNDO·QUOD USTI·FOEDERA·SERVET
SPERNAT·DAMNATUM·VI CAT·PIETATE·DOLORUM
CUT·FAUOR·ATQTIMORV· RT·ACTUAL·MA·CORONA·ES

PULCHRIORES·TOTO·VE NAUT·FLORIBUS·ARUO
CELSIORA·CCEDRO·PAR OET·PRECIO·CTOR·ALBO
QUADRATAS·IUNGIS·IN IRMO·TRAMITE·PETRAS
ET·RI·DE·PARTE·ACO·HAR IUS·PLEBSQUE·OR·IORA
FUND·A·MENTA·TRAHITI FUN·Q·DOMATIS·OMUIS
QUAE·E·CUE·DE·NOTA·COR ACC·T·DOGMATE·PRIMU
VIUO·E·RETECTUME·EGV NTRU·ERBA·PROPHETAE
COMPL·QUERANT·VIDAMI PERIS·AULA·PI·REGI·
YT·CR·STORA·FORMAS·S UNT·VLCAMMATE·RITO
OMNIS·NAMQ·SIMUS·CRA DIT·BNOMEWAD·ASTRA
HAEC·AULA·IESUS·OLA· TUMS·VLMI·VISA·CTON
ET·VO·FIRMATA·IGE BONA·STRUCTIO·ITAE
IUNC·VO·LIGNA·AT·H ECO·MNE·ULLO·MCARE
QUA·VIA·QUE·DUCIT·AD CISSCEPTRA·TENENDA
QUOS·TEMPLO·DEDICAT AETA·BONA·MANSIG·XPI
QUATTUORAT·Q·CRUCIS UGET·CUM·RUPIBUS·TIS·
PERFECTAM·Q·DOMUM·D DUCENS·ANGULUS·IPSE

Some wondered if an angel could recognize other angels or even know itself. (Aquinas: "The angels do not know their own power perfectly; according as it proceeds from the order of the Divine Wisdom, which to the angels is incomprehensible.") Gregory of Nyssa in the 4th century had called angels "rational animals," but Aquinas said that "since the intellectual light is perfect in the angel, for he is a pure and most clear mirror. . . it follows that the angel does not understand by reasoning."

Augustine had said that, in heaven "our thoughts will not be fleeting, going and returning from one thing to another, but we shall survey all our knowledge at the same time by one glance," so it was presumed that angels have this understanding. Some said they were given universal knowledge at the moment of their creation, but are unable to learn anything new or specific. (Isidore of Seville in the 7th century, however, said that "demons learn more things by experience.") Others said that since they have universal knowledge, they don't need to learn anything new.

Whether they remember anything at all was resolved by Aquinas with a mis-citation: "Isidore says that the angels have learnt many things by experience. But experience comes of many remembrances, as stated in [Aristotle]. Consequently they have likewise a power of memory."

The angels, in fact, could be oddly ignorant. Christians tended to read everything in the Old Testament—from isolated phrases out of context to the physical lovers of the Song of Songs—as prophecies or literal or allegorical descriptions of the events that were to occur in the New Testament. Justin Martyr and Irenaeus in the 2nd century and Athanasius of Alexandria in the 4th century took a few lines from Psalm 24—"Who is this King of glory? The Lord of hosts, he is the King of glory"—and realized that this was a scene from the Ascension of Jesus: The bewildered heavenly angels are asking the angels accompanying Jesus who this human is. Origen, and Ambrose and Gregory Nazianzen and Gregory of Nyssa in the 4th century then added two questions to the dialogue, taken from a poem in Isaiah on the vengeance of Yahweh: "Who is this coming from Edom, from Bozrah in garments stained with crimson? Why are your garments red, your clothes as if you had trodden the winepress?" (The red stains become the blood from the Crucifixion—tradition maintains that Jesus kept his wounds open even in heaven. Bozrah is not the bloodstained Basra of the Iraq War.) The explanation for why the angels had never heard of the Son of God is that the Ascension was a revelation of the Mystery equally for humans and angels.

Aquinas somewhat explains:

> There is a twofold knowledge in the angel. The first is his natural knowledge, according to which he knows things both by his essence, and by innate species. By such knowledge the angels cannot know mysteries of grace. For these mysteries depend upon the pure will of God: and if an angel cannot learn the thoughts of another angel, which depend upon the will of such angel, much less can he ascertain what depends entirely upon God's will. . . [Angels] know mysteries of grace, but not all mysteries: nor do they all know them equally.

Nevertheless, even assuming the unknowability of God, it is equally a mystery that he never told the angels about his son. The exegetes avoided the question.

The space and time that angels inhabit is controversial. As they are not material, they cannot occupy any space. Aquinas said they are capable of moving from place to place in an instant. (Thomas Shepard in the 17th century, anticipating Superman, said that angels fly "swifter than a Bullet from a Musket.") But, according to Aquinas, they could not be in two places at the same time. Less certain, among others, was whether two angels could be in the same place at the same time. (This was later parodied by Protestants as the typically Scholastic debate of how many angels can dance on the head of a pin.) Aquinas denied it. However, he was unusually noncommittal on the question of whether an angel, moving instantly from place to place, travels through the intermediate space. He said sometimes they do and sometimes they don't, according to their will.

Although some say there is an obscure class of angels called the Ephemerae, who live only for a day and expire after chanting the *Te Deum*, the rest of the angels do not age or decay and are not subject to material time; there are no images of elderly angels. As only God can be eternal, the medieval scholars invented a word for the duration of the angels: an *aeviternity*. The eternity of God has no beginning or end; the aeviternity had a beginning and may not have an end. (Bonaventure, however, dissented: as partially material created creatures they must have an end.) In any event, angels exist for a very long time, and this longevity is comforting. According to Henry Latham, an Anglican theologian in the 19th century, "We feel less ephemeral when we have made friends with an Angel who saw the pterodactyl's first attempt at flying, or who, possibly, put the notion into his head."

Angels apparently have no individual personalities or qualities; none have ever been noted. In the canonical Bible, only Gabriel and Michael are named. In other passages, following the desert rules of hospitality, the humans often ask the angels their names, but the angels refuse to answer. Later, some believed that this was because the true names of the angels are too complicated for human comprehension. Others said that the angels have no names, that God never named them, nor did the angels name themselves; the names we know are human inventions. According to Meister Eckhart in the 13th century, Gabriel's name "was no more Gabriel than it was Conrad. No one can know an angel's name. No master and no mind have ever penetrated to a place where an angel is known by name, and perhaps indeed it has no name. The soul too is nameless." The rabbi Rashi in the 11th century, echoing Gregory of Nyssa, said that angels have no fixed names, but that their "names change according to the command of the task of the mission on which they are sent," rather like spies.

It is debatable whether these nameless beings have a will of their own. They are supposed to be the pure expressions and instruments of God's will, and yet some of them rebelled. Meister Eckhart said that "If God told an angel to go to a tree and pluck caterpillars off it, the angel would be quite ready to do so, and it would be his happiness, if it were the will of God." Aquinas summarizes the case against free will:

> The act of free will is to choose. But there can be no choice with the angels, because choice is "the desire of something after taking counsel," while counsel is "a kind of inquiry," as stated in [Aristotle]. But the angels' knowledge is not the result of inquiring, for this belongs to the discursiveness of reason. Therefore it appears that there is no free will in the angels.

In his own conclusion, however, he counters it weakly: "On the contrary, free will is part of man's dignity. But the angels' dignity surpasses that of men. Therefore, since free will is in men, with much more reason is it in the angels."

Their emotional life is impenetrable. Because of their proximity to God, they exist in eternal (or aeviternal) joy, but traditionally they wept at the Crucifixion and grieve for the sins of man. According to Aquinas: "Where there is grief and sorrow, there is not perfect happiness. . . But the angels are perfectly happy. Therefore they have no cause for grief." Some commentators asked if angels have amicable affections for one another. (On the one hand, as beings of love, how could they not? On the other, as beings with no individuality, how could they?) According to Luke, even one sinner who repents brings joy to the angels, which raised the question among the scholars of whether an angel could feel more joy than it already has.

In fact, the simplicity of angels could be vexing. Mechthilde of Magdeburg in the 13th century said that "angels are simple persons and they do not praise God nor love him nor know him beyond the limits of their nature. The least of human beings can catch up with them." In the holy eroticism of her visions, she wrote that she could take Jesus "in my arms, eat him and drink him, and have my way with him. This can never happen to the angels." "What, then," she added disdainfully, "do I care what the angels experience?"

By the time of the Renaissance, humanists such as Nicholas of Cusa in the 15th century were arguing that the diversity of human individuals collectively formed a microcosm of the universe that ultimately would become one with the complexity of God, in ways that the angels could not. God therefore chose to send a god-man to earth and not an angel to begin this reconciliation.

The origin of the angels is unknown. They are not mentioned in Genesis as beings created at the Creation. Augustine said that they fall under the rubric of "heavens" ("the heavens and the earth") or "light" ("let there be light"). Others said they were created before the material universe. The Fourth Lateran Council of 1215 decreed that God "from the beginning of time created both orders of creation in the same way, that is, the angelic order and the earthly." Calvin dismissed the speculation: "To stir up questions concerning the time and order in which they were created bespeaks more perverseness than industry."

Angels cannot produce more angels; presumably only God can create them and there is no indication, except among certain Kabbalists, that he has created others after the initial group. Those Kabbalists claimed that God creates more angels with every breath he exhales, which assumes that God breathes. There are folkloric beliefs and individual beliefs among the mystics that the souls of saints or babies or of the just become angels, but the institutional dogma is more complicated. Tertullian in the 3rd century said that with the Second Coming of Christ the bodies of the faithful will be resurrected and Christ will reign for a thousand years in a New Jerusalem built by God. At the end of that time, the people will rise to heaven, become angels, and occupy the empty seats of those who fell with Satan. This was accepted as true, but raised questions that were debated for centuries: Will the resurrected bodies of the maimed or mutilated be restored to wholeness? How old will they be? Will the bodies be bodies as we now know them, subject to the temptations of the flesh, or a new kind of pure body? (In which case, are they really human bodies?) Where are the souls of the just between now and the endtime, if not in heaven? (Exceptions were made for the martyred saints, who went directly to heaven.) Tertullian wrote a book called *About Paradise*—the first in Latin on the subject—which perhaps held some answers, but it has been lost.

Jesus said that angels do not marry, but Milton's angels have sex. In *Paradise Lost*, Adam asks Raphael whether they express their love "by looks only, or do they mix / Irradiance, virtual or immediate touch?" Raphael, blushing "celestial rosy red," replies:

> . . . Let it suffice thee that thou know'st
> Us happy, and without Love no happiness.
> Whatever pure thou in the body enjoy'st
> (And pure thou wert created) we enjoy
> In eminence, and obstacle find none
> Of membrane, joint, or limb, exclusive bars:
> Easier than Air with Air, if Spirits embrace,
> Total they mix, Union of Pure with Pure
> Desiring; nor restrain'd conveyance need
> As Flesh to mix with Flesh, or Soul with Soul.

He quickly changes the subject: "But I can now no more. . . the parting sun. . . sets, my signal to depart." (Milton coincides with his contemporary Henry More, who wrote that angels reap "the lawful pleasures of the very Animal life, in a far higher degree then we are capable of in this World." Whereas in the terrestrial world, "the judicious Eye cannot but espy some considerable defect in either the proportion, color, or the air of the face, in the most famed and most admired beauties of either Sex," the angels "cannot but enravish one another's Souls, while they are mutual Spectators of the perfect pulchritude of one another's persons, and comely carriage.")

Moreover, although Raphael doesn't mention it, Milton describes the angels as gender-fluid:

> For spirits when they please
> Can either sex assume, or both; so soft
> And uncompounded is their essence pure,
> Not tied or manacled with joint or limb,
> Nor founded on the brittle strength of bones,
> Like cumbrous flesh; but in what shape they choose

OMNIAIAMSPLENDENTVERODELVMINECRISTI
INLVSTRATACRVCISETSACRAEFACTABEANDO
CONCELEBRANTVICTORISICVOTASVPERNO
DEBITAPERSOLVANTDEVOTEREGNACANENTES
CVNCTATENEREMODVMSVBMAGNONVMINEIESV
QVICQVIDINORBEMEATEDACISIVICQIDVBIQ
ESTSAPITETSENTITVIVITETIVRARESERVAT
HOCTERRAPONTVSHOCSIDERAGRAMINAVENTI
IMPERIOSVBERVNTHOCSVNTANTEGEFVERVNT
IMBERNVBSGRANDOGLACIESNIXATGEPRVINA
FONTESETRIVIPVLVISETROSIVBARABSQHOC
CRETAGARGONACTVSTELLACATQVELAERGGE
ENALMVMETNONVADAROROMRSVSDICITEVERA
ACMODVLOSCANTVSODASCANTETQVOQVEIVST
OMNIACRVXTRAXATETSANOPIEIVRECORONET
LAVDEDEINONDISCORDETSEDDICATHONESTA
IVSOPVSCAVDENSPISCESDIRIGEDRACONE
COLLESETLVCIMONTESPECORAARBOSHAREN
CVMQEFERISVESPAEVERMESETBESTIARICT
ETPLACIDAEVVLTVSEVSEVAMENTEVOLVCRES
RISTICOLAEQSAVLAPOLITERRAQSATAFIT
VOISGIRTLVMENDVCENSVNDIQVEADHOSTES
NVNTIAFERTPREXEITAVTVNDASEDOREPERIT
FAMAIQEMAXABICITPALMAMNOSCIHICRAPTO
DATFELICIDATIVSTISHAECCVNTIACVNCTIS
PARCENSRITEHOSTIDATFATVVIVEREMVLTOS
SEDIVREDAMNATQVOSAVCTVSSEPSITITINIQVS
INDEDECETPARITERORAVMNITZANTIALAVDES
VOTAQDECLAMENTGRATESGENVESTRAPOLORVM
TVRBAETTVPOPVLVSQVEMPROFERTTELLVBIQ
VOSRATIOCONSORSPARITERDIREXITADODAS
CAVDIAVOSCAELICAELESTIAREGNABONAQVE
IAMSORTECAPIVNTETVOTISVALDEGERIRVNT
ENDEDITHOCVESTERVOBISSALVATORETIPSE
REXPROPRIVSPRAESVLLETQVECREATORIESVS

Dilated or condens'd, bright or obscure,
Can execute their aerie purposes,
And works of love or enmity fulfil.

In Genesis, certain angels, who are male and have been given the evocative name The Watchers, find the daughters of men alluring and marry "as many as they chose." Their offspring may or not be the race of giants known as the Nephilim. This takes place before the Flood, and yet, long after, when supposedly only Noah's descendants are left on earth, Moses sends some spies into Canaan, and they encounter the Nephilim. They report: "to ourselves we seemed like grasshoppers and so we seemed to them." Later commentators would debate whether these marrying angels were the ones from heaven or fallen ones. The requirement that women keep their heads covered in church was to prevent the angels, looking down, from temptation. As Origen pointed out, whenever the faithful gather in prayer, there is necessarily an equal number of guardian angels, one for each individual, watching over.

The angels who succumbed to temptation, the devils, according to Origen, "multiply like flies." "They move among us," said Francisco Blasco Lanuza in the 17th century, "thicker than the atoms we see in rays of sunshine. . . those unimaginable specks to be seen when a ray of sun enters through a window." Johann Weyer, the Dutch demonologist in the 16th century, said there are exactly 7,409,127 devils. Others calculated 1,758,064,176 (6 legions of demons containing 66 cohorts each with 666 companies of 6,666 individuals.) Others simply multiplied the palindromic Pythagorean number 1,234,321 times 6 to arrive at 7,405,926. The followers of Luther estimated their number at 2.5 billion, then raised the figure to 10 trillion—roughly 100,000 devils for every Christian at the time of the Reformation, creating nearly infinite possibilities for iniquities.

(Jewish demons, the shedim, are "more numerous than we are" and are composed of fire and air, whereas Jewish angels are composed of fire and ice. They are invisible, have wings and fly. Like angels, they know the future—but they only know the immediate future and they only know it by eavesdropping on the real angels. They help explain the inexplicable: why, for example, the clothes of a scholar who does nothing but read become worn: the shedim are continually rubbing up against him. One can see them by eating the roasted and minced placenta of a purebred black cat, but to speak of what one has seen may be fatal. Moses Maimonides in the 12th century doubted they existed.)

Demons, unlike angels, are almost always described as extremely intelligent. Augustine says that they "with the greatest faculty learn man's dispositions, not only when expressed by speech, but even when conceived in thought, when the soul expresses them by certain signs in the body." Moreover, "it cannot be asserted how this is done."

And unlike angels, they are psychologically astute. Blasco Lanuza delineated seven modes of temptation, corresponding to the seven-headed dragon of Revelation: *Importuna* ("continuous importuning"); *Dubia* ("when doubts are created"); *Subita* ("a sudden temptation, which, being so sudden, admits of neither deliberation or reason"); *Oculta* ("which is so secret its malice cannot be overcome by reason"); *Violenta* ("the will is violated by fear of death or serious harm and so consents"); *Perplexa* (when one finds oneself caught between two evils and "does not know how to choose the lesser"); and *Fraudulenta* ("when the will is deceived by the appearance of what is good and just").

To complicate matters, Christian demons are able to assume the bodies of angels, "to transform themselves into Angels of Light," in the words of Increase Mather, echoing Paul in 2 Corinthians. Worse, according to Mather, they are scientifically advanced: "How easy then is it for Daemons, who have a perfect Understanding in Opticks, and in the Power of Nature to deceive the Eyes and delude the Imaginations of Silly Mortals." In the countless witch trials in Europe, many of those who were hanged or burnt at the stake said they had met with an angel, and only under extreme torture admitted that their angel was actually a demon.

The origin of those demons in the rebellion of the angels was difficult to understand. Augustine said "there is in the holy angels that nature which cannot sin," and obviously (in the words of Aquinas) God did not "create the angelic nature imperfect and incomplete." Aquinas explained that there were actually two stages in the creation of the angels:

> According to Augustine, the growing of plants from the earth did not take place at once among the first works, in which only the germinating power of the plants was bestowed upon the earth. In the same way, the angelic creature in the beginning of its existence had the perfection of its nature; but it did not have the perfection to which it had to come by its operation.
>
> The angel has a twofold knowledge of the Word; the one which is natural, and the other according to glory. He has a natural knowledge whereby he knows the Word through a similitude thereof shining in his nature; and he has a knowledge of glory whereby he knows the Word through His essence. By both kinds of knowledge the angel knows things in the Word; imperfectly by his natural knowledge, and perfectly by his knowledge of glory. Therefore the first knowledge of things in the Word was present to the angel from the outset of his creation; while the second was not, but only when the angels became blessed by turning to the good.

After the first stage and before the second, the angels could succumb to sin, but they were only the "spiritual" sins of pride and envy and not the carnal ones. As Augustine said, the devil "is not a fornicator nor a drunkard, nor anything of the like sort." Aquinas elaborated: "The demons do not delight in the obscenities of the sins of the flesh, as if they themselves were disposed to carnal pleasures: it is wholly through envy that they take pleasure in all sorts of human sins, so far as these are hindrances to a man's good." In other versions, the envy of the rebel angels was directed not at human sins, in which they were incapable of indulging, but at the adulation of Jesus, Adam (at the Creation), and even God himself.

It is confusing exactly when the rebellion occurred. Some say before the Creation; some say after. Jesus—who only once mentions the "eternal fire prepared for the devil and his angels"—says that he "watched Satan fall like lightning." Perhaps this was before his earthly existence. The only Biblical account of the rebellion—apart from a few words in passing from Peter and Jude—is in a mere three lines in Revelation. (Much of *Paradise Lost* is essentially an extrapolation of those three lines.) Revelation is a kind of hallucinatory collage of previous Biblical imagery, where even the locusts wear gold crowns and iron breastplates, have human faces, the hair of women, and the tails of scorpions. But it is clearly intended to be a vision of the future: "things which must shortly come to pass." Either the fall of the angels has not yet happened, or it will happen again, or past and future dissolve at the apocalyptic end of time.

In the Hebrew Bible, the eternal war between God and Satan, first imagined by the Zoroastrians, is unknown. Satan ("the Adversary") only appears three times. He is an angel, but possibly not a fallen one, because he seemingly works for God. His job is prosecutorial: presenting evidence of an individual's sins to the divine court of judgment. In the indelible line in Job, he gathers his evidence "From going to and fro in the earth, and from walking up and down in it." In Revelation, he is a dragon. Christians would later conflate him with Lucifer, the "bringer of light," who is normally Venus as the morning star, because of a passage in Isaiah ("How art thou fallen from heaven, O Lucifer, son of the morning!") which was originally about the King of Babylon. In the 1360s, amidst the Black Plague, the traditional Christian interpretation of Isaiah as a prophecy of the coming of Christ was revealed to be a prophecy of the coming of Konrad Schmid, the new Messiah. His followers, the Secret Flagellants of Thuringia, considered the Church itself the Antichrist of Revelation, and awaited the coming End of Days by scourging themselves, and being scourged by their Messiah. Newborn babies were baptized by being beaten until they bled. Schmid was burned at the stake, but the cult lasted for a hundred years, protected by an angel apparently also inspired by Isaiah: Its name was Venus.

Although never explicitly delineated in the Bible, Christians assumed that, before the arrival of Jesus on earth, everything humans knew about the cosmos had been explained to them by angels: "Abraham," said Clement of Alexandria in the 2nd century, "was initiated into the secrets of God by an angel." He also believed that it was the angels who had taught the Greeks philosophy. Origen extended this to the Egyptian mysteries, Chaldean astrology, and even the "Hindu claims pertaining to the science of the Most High God." Moses received the Law, not directly from Yahweh, but through angelic intermediaries, who, according to Augustine, "proclaimed the Law with an awesome voice."

The angels, however, were not up to their tasks. As John Chrysostom in the 4th century said, "God set all things in motion through the angels, and nothing was working out well." The angels had failed: sin and idolatry were rampant, even among the Chosen People of Israel. So God sent his son to earth to assume the pedagogical role of spreading the True Word. Yet, to the consternation of the Apostles, humans remained attached to the angels, who were too often venerated almost as little gods. Paul, in the letter to the Colossians, writes (in the straightforward translation of the *Jerusalem Bible*): "Do not be taken in by people who like groveling to angels and worshiping them; people like that are always going on about some vision they have had, inflating themselves to a false importance with their worldly outlook." In the Letter to the Hebrews—which at one time was believed to have been written by Paul—it says bluntly: "God has never said to any angel, 'You are my Son.'"

The Church then redefined the angels as merely the helpmates and celebrants of Jesus. Augustine spelled it out:

> The message of [the City of God] is proclaimed by the holy angels, who have invited our attention to their society and who desire us to be with them in this city. For these angels do not in any way aspire to our worship of them as gods, but that we dwell with them, attentive only to their God and ours. Nor do they desire us to sacrifice to them, but that with them we should be a sacrifice to God.

Protestants never quite knew what to do with angels. Their existence and their services to humankind were Scriptural and could not be denied; but the preoccupation with them was dismissed as popery. As Calvin said, "One God is better than a universe of angels."

2.

Augustine said that angels are gardeners: God created the plants—that is, us—and the angels tend them. In the Bible there is no evidence of this. The angels mainly deliver messages from God; the words in Hebrew and Greek, *ma'lak* and *angelos*, mean "messenger." In the most familiar stories, they tell Abraham not to sacrifice Isaac, or Mary that she is pregnant. It was later believed that angels also deliver the prayers of the faithful to God; and still later, in Protestantism, that this was not true. The assumption that angels escort the souls of good people to heaven —the source of all the angelic statuary in cemeteries—was derived from a single line in the Bible: In the parable of the rich man and the beggar Lazarus, Jesus says that "the beggar died, and was carried by the angels into Abraham's bosom."

An angel helps Peter escape prison, but they are otherwise only occasionally benevolent in the Bible. Angels are warriors. When King David inexplicably incurs the wrath of Yahweh by ordering a census, an angel sends a plague that kills 70,000 people to diminish the count. Another angel destroys the entire army of Sennacherib, king of Assyria, in a single night. Another, who again may or may not be Yahweh himself, pointlessly wrestles all night with Jacob. An angel smites Herod, who is eaten by worms. (But it is Yahweh, not an "angel of death," who slays the first-born of Egypt in Exodus.) They are often depicted in battle gear. Martin Luther in the 16th century: "I believe that the angels are all up in arms, are putting on their harness, and girding their swords about them. For the Last Judgment draws nigh, and the angels prepare themselves for the combat, and to strike down Turk and Pope into the bottomless pit."

The kinder guardian angels seem to owe their discovery to two lines in Psalm 91 ("For he shall give his angels charge over thee, to keep thee in all ways. / They shall bear thee up in their hands, lest thou dash thy foot against a stone"—lines repeated by the devil when he takes Jesus to the "pinnacle of the temple" and challenges him to jump off—and to a single word in a single line in Matthew, where Jesus says, "Take heed that ye despise not one of these little ones [i.e., the children], for . . . in heaven *their* angels do always behold the face of my Father which is in heaven." They were otherwise unknown until after the Bible was written. According to Aquinas, "all corporeal things are governed by angels"; according to Augustine, "every visible thing in this world is put under the charge of an angel"; according to Basil of Caesarea in the 4th century, they "guard the soul like an army"; according to the Talmud, this includes an angel for each blade of grass, encouraging it to grow; according to Luther, "when you see that a stable, a village, a house still stands, that is a sign that the angels protect us." Bernard of Clairvaux exclaimed, "How buoyantly someone swims when another is holding up his chin!" Some, however, wondered why God, who neither slumbers nor sleeps as he watches over all of us, would need the assistance of the guardian angels.

Christians debated whether every human has one, assigned at birth or in the womb—though some said the fetus was protected by the mother's angel—or whether only Christians were given one at baptism. Aquinas said that indeed everyone initially has a guardian angel, but it only begins to guard after baptism. Luther said that there have always been guardian angels for all, even among the pagans: their interventions were merely once attributed to "good fortune," not knowing that the reason "that such things happened" was because "the true God had done them through His holy angels." A particularly thorny question was whether Adam had a guardian angel before the Fall, while he was still in paradise, when presumably he wouldn't need one. (Aquinas said he did: Adam himself was in a state of innocence within, but was threatened by the snares of demons without.) Unfortunately, it was generally agreed that every person also has been assigned an evil angel by Satan, one who inspires thoughts and acts of wickedness. Individuals live torn between the two angels. Luther and the Protestants tended to be preoccupied with the evil ones.

According to Blasco Lanuza, the guardian angels have twelve tasks: to teach us, to mediate between us and God, to prevent dangers, to fight against the devil, to reprimand us, to console us, to guide us, to reduce our temptations, to defend us, to help us out of predicaments, to exhort us to virtue, and to lovingly punish us. Christopher Smart in the 18th century put it more simply: "My Angel is always ready at a pinch to help me out and to keep me up." Francesco Albertini in the 17th century said they help us with the seven principal miseries where "we stand in need of assistance": folly (being primarily sensuality), hastiness, dullness, fear, ignorance, pride, and lack of feeling. They see everything; they move mountains and the heavenly spheres; they travel with a "speed of angelic motion [that] surpasses our imagination," they never grow tired. Although they witness everything we do, they cannot read our thoughts. However, they sometimes ask God what we are thinking.

It was questioned how the guardian angels can advise when human suffering may be beyond their understanding, certainly beyond their experience, and when they are apparently incapable of grasping a new situation. Moreover, the guardian angels seem to frequently neglect their duties, allowing accidents to happen, feet to be dashed against stones, and temptations to succeed. This, said Aquinas, was not due to "the negligence of the angels but to the malice of men."

It was unclear how the angels divided their time between serving God in heaven and protecting their wards on earth. John of Damascus had clearly stated that "when the angels are here with us, they are not in heaven." Conversely, if they were in heaven at a certain moment, were they then forsaking us? Aquinas, as usual, had the answer:

> Although an angel may forsake a man sometimes locally, he does not for that reason forsake him as to the effect of his guardianship: for even when he is in heaven he knows what is happening to man; nor does he need time for his local motion, for he can be with man in an instant.

The medieval scholars wondered how guardian angels feel about their charges, if they do: Are they proud of achievements and ashamed of sins, or do they exist literally above it all, in a kind of benevolent detachment? Others believed that they merely keep their wards under surveillance, recording the good and bad deeds for a final report after the ward's death, which would determine admission to heaven or hell. As Increase Mather said, "Remember, that the Angels are the Spectators of your Behavior. Behave your selves, as having the Eyes of the Angels on you. Often think, Is not an Angel standing by?"

```
CHRISTUSSALUATORCRI | STUSREXARCESERENUS
CONSILIUMUIRTUSMAG  | AETBENEDICTIOLUMEN
PATRISDIUINAPROLES  | ERTETRAHITOMNEHINC
IUSORTUMFACTURAFAB  | UMMOSCASTUSHONOREM
HINCQUEBONUMQICQID  | ERUMMIRUMQUIDETUR
IUSTITIAEQICQUIDARC | AEQUICQUIDMANETORBE
QUICQUIDRITEPROBAT  | TPROFERTORDINEMUND;
ANGELUSATQ:BONUSQAE | AMSUFFERTETINIQUUS
SUNTHINCQUODQEDEUS  | ANUMDEIECERATEXHOC
SAECLOIUSREUOCANS   | OMNIACRISTUSHONORE
COHPLECTITDOMINANS  | CONSIGNATMUNERANU
HINCDECETUTGENUSHU  | ANUMETLUMINISEXSUL
NORETHOSRADIOSQUOS  | RICITHAECBENEDICTA
CRUXSALUANSETREDDE  | SQEMIAMPRIMHABEBAT
ECSORTUMLUCISNOCUU  | QUOABSCESSERATADAM
QOTQOTIAMRADIOSUER  | ENISTOSCELEBRABANT
PERPETUALUCISFULGE  | CUNTSORTECREBROQUE
HOCCANDORESATISMIC  | ERUNTARMAPROPHETAE

GREXETAPOSTOLICUSDECORATURLUCECORUSCA

HOCQ:FIDESCHRISTICA  | DETHOCSOLERELUCENT
CORDABENEHOMINUMUO   | TAQUOLUMINECLISCUNT
IUSTIPOLLENTESPERM   | STICASIGNABONUMQUE
CONICIENTRADIUMMAN   | DATISCREDEREOBIPSUM
ETTRIBUUNTPOPULISCU  | MIURASUPERNAHOTARE
ADSCRIBUNTCHRISTOCO  | NSORTIADUCEREUITAE
CHRISTUSREXDOMINUS   | DIUINUSMUNERESUMMUS
SCANDENSALTACRUCIS   | NROBORAFUNDITIINHOC
ISTAMTUNCSPECIEPL    | TANDOPANDERECAELOS
TRADIDITETUOLUIT     | TOSCONQUIRIERILLIC
ERGOQATERTERNOSABA   | QUARUMETLIMITEMUNDI
HOCUENTOSINCALLECRU  | UCISBENEDIXERATIPSE
SIGNAQ:BISSENAPRINC  | PSSTIPANDOGUBERNAT
ACDUODENASUIORIEN    | SPLAGASUSCIPITHORIS
TRACTADIEISPATIENHI  | ISSECTITOTALABORAT
OMNIANAMCRISTICRUX   | GLORIASEPTARESOLUT
IPSAQ:SANCTAPOLIST   | SGAUDIAIURAQ:TERRAE
PROPONITSIGNATLAUD   | TPROBATIPSAQEDONAT
```

Catherine of Siena in the 14th century at age six could see guardian angels as clearly as people. The guardian angel of Isidore the Farmer in the 12th century would do his ploughing for him while he prayed. The guardian angel of Mary Frances of the Five Wounds in the 18th century taught her "how to defend herself against the assaults of her father's anger." Less sympathetic, the guardian angel of Birgitta of Sweden, in the 14th century, told God: "She has a big and conceited heart. Therefore she needs the rod in order to be tamed." God said: "What is your request for her, my friend?" The angel replied: "Lord, I ask you to grant her mercy along with the rod." And God said: "For your sake, I will do so, since I never perform justice without mercy. This is why the bride should love me with all her heart."

Both the Polish Maria Faustyna Kowalska in the 20th century and the Dutch Lidwina of Schiedam in the 15th century visited purgatory—which was invented in the 12th century as an actual place—accompanied by their guardian angels. Faustyna saw "a misty place full of fire in which there was a great crowd of suffering souls. They were praying fervently, but to no avail, for themselves; only we can come to their aid." (That is, those in purgatory are only released through the prayers of those on earth.) Most remarkably, "I saw Our Lady visiting the souls in purgatory. The souls call her 'The Star of the Sea.' She brings them refreshment."

Lidwina, who was severely handicapped by an ice skating accident as a teenager, had converted a sinful man through her prayers, but he died soon after, unable to do penance. Her guardian angel took her to visit him in purgatory, where she met another guardian angel, and which her hagiography recounts in a style reminiscent of Lovecraft:

> She saw what resembled an immense prison surrounded with walls of a prodigious height, the blackness of which, together with the monstrous stones, inspired her with horror. Approaching this dismal enclosure, she heard a confused noise of lamenting voices, cries of fury, chains, instruments of torture, violent blows which the executioners discharged upon their victims. This noise was such that all the tumult of the world, in tempest

or battle, could bear no comparison to it. "What, then, is that horrible place?" asked St. Lidwina of her good angel. "Do you wish me to show it to you?" "No, I beseech you," said she, recoiling with terror, "the noise I hear is so frightful that I can no longer bear it; how, then, could I endure the sight of those horrors?"

Continuing her mysterious route, she saw an angel seated sadly on the curb of a well. "Who is that angel?" she asked of her guide. "It is," he replied, "the angel-guardian of the sinner in whose lot you are interested. His soul is in this well, where it has a special purgatory." At these words Lidwina cast an inquiring glance at her angel; she desired to see that soul which was dear to her, and endeavor to release it from that frightful pit. Her angel, who understood her, having taken off the cover of the well, a cloud of flames, together with the most plaintive cries, came forth. "Do you recognize that voice?" said the angel to her. "Alas! yes," answered the servant of God. "Do you desire to see that soul?" he continued. On her replying in the affirmative, he called him by his name; and immediately our virgin saw appear at the mouth of the pit a spirit all on fire, resembling incandescent metal, which said to her in a voice scarcely audible, "O Lidwina, servant of God, who will give me to contemplate the face of the Most High?" The sight of this soul, a prey to the most terrible torment of fire, gave our saint such a shock that the cincture which she wore around her body was rent in twain; and, no longer able to endure the sight, she awoke suddenly from her ecstasy.

Some days later, the same angel whom she had seen so dejected appeared to her with a joyful countenance; he told her that the soul of his protégé had left the pit and passed into the ordinary purgatory. This partial alleviation did not suffice the charity of Lidwina; she continued to pray for the poor patient, and to apply to him the merits of her sufferings, until she saw the gates of heaven opened to him.

Gemma Galgani, the Flower of Lucca, died in 1903 at the age of 25. Every Thursday evening she would fall into a rapture and receive the stigmata. She was in the "constant sight" of her guardian angel. According to her confessor, she "saw him with her eyes, touched him with her hand as if he were a being of this world, remained talking with him as one friend with another. . . . The angel sometimes let her see him raised in the air with outspread wings, his hands extended over her or joined in an attitude of prayer. At other times, he knelt beside her. . . . I noted that every time she raised her eyes to look at the angel, listen to him, or speak to him. . . she lost the use of her senses. At those moments one could prick, burn, or shake her without her feeling it." Gemma was demanding. "She kept the heavenly messenger continually on the move," delivering letters for her to people all over the world. Her angel even brought her coffee in bed during her many illnesses.

In 1830, in a convent of the Daughters of Charity on the Rue du Bac in Paris, occurred the first of many modern worldwide apparitions of the Virgin Mary. July 18th was the Feast Day of Vincent de Paul, the founder of the order, and the nuns were given pieces of the saint's vestments to swallow before they went to sleep. Just before midnight, Catherine Labouré, a young novitiate, was awakened by the voice of a child calling to her. He was about four years old and dressed in white. "Get up quickly and go to the chapel; the Blessed Virgin is waiting for you. . . Come, I will guard you."

As they walked through the corridors, candles miraculously lit, and the boy himself radiated multicolored light. A locked door opened at his touch. They entered the chapel, which was also brightly lit with candles. They waited, and then she heard a rustling of silk and the boy said, "See the Virgin here, see the Virgin here. Look at the Virgin." Then his voice changed to that of a man: "Can not the Queen of Heaven appear at random to a poor mortal creature in the way she pleases?"

Catherine and the Virgin spoke for two hours; the Virgin warned her of impending political chaos in France. According to her hagiography, "Catherine received many messages from the lips of the Blessed Virgin Mary, but we cannot know all of them, because some were given with the command of absolute secret."

In the 20th century, Maria Valtorta offered herself as a "victim to Divine Justice." At age thirty-seven she became paralyzed and remained in bed for the next twenty-seven years, until her death in 1961. There she wrote "The Poem of the Man-God," a detailed description of the life and times of Jesus, based entirely on her visions, which is 10,000 pages long. Her guardian angel, who was named Azariah, also dictated to her 5000 pages of Biblical commentary and biographies of the early martyrs, but unfortunately her writings are on the Vatican list of forbidden books.

Veronica Giuliani, a Capuchin nun in the 18th century, was so often attacked by the devil (in the form of a cat) that the Virgin Mary appointed a second guardian angel to protect her. They both accompanied her on frequent visits to hell and purgatory. Once, kneeling before a crucifix, the left arm of Jesus detached and embraced her. Her hagiography notes:

> An autopsy was performed on Veronica the day of her death after lunch. During her lifetime, Veronica had told Blessed Florida that her heart bore certain symbols of the Passion and that it had been engraved with the letters representing the vows she had taken. Blessed Florida made a sketch of her heart with all the signs that Veronica described. When her heart was dissected in half during the autopsy, it revealed mysterious incisions shaped like the outlines of the instruments of the Passion, the seven swords of Our Lady, and a number of letters.

God revealed to Veronica Giuliani that, upon the election of a new Pope, heaven appoints to him an additional ten guardian angels to assist him. Pope John XXIII in the 20th century, however, seems to have had only one. But, practiced in the ways of both heavenly and terrestrial power, he made active use of his angel:

> Whenever we have to speak with someone who is rather closed to our argument and with whom therefore the conversations need to be very persuasive, we go to our guardian angel. We recommend

the matter to him. We ask him to take it up with the guardian angel of the person we have to see. And once the two angels establish an understanding, the Pope's conversation with his visitor is much easier.

In a disconcerting revelation, the astronomer Robert Browne in the 18th century writes:

> Once in the Night, being restless, I fell upon some Divine Meditations, and devout Ejaculations to God, till I became Heavenly inclined; and earnestly desired some visible or sensible Appearance of my good Guardian Angel; upon which, thinking I perceived some rushing about the Bed, I became surprised, and was immediately transposed as in a Dream, and then perceived something with much tranquility of Mind slide into the Bed, which represented a naked Child, it seemed to embrace me, I imagined that I took hold of its Hands and Feet, which felt extremely soft and pleasant, and in a secret sort of Speech I said art thou come, and it secretly answered yes; upon which I recovered my self with much satisfaction, & c.

On a later night, the angel Gabriel appears "in a thin white Garment, his upper parts naked, in the Form of a Man about 50 with a pale white Countenance, and a short comely Beard." Browne asks for his guardian angel, but Gabriel says he is "abroad upon other occasions." Browne then asks to be told his angel's name. Letters appear, but when he wakes up he can't remember them.

3.

Angels are the largely anonymous workers in the hive of heaven, fulfilling functions in the army or in the royal court. They inhabit the celestial spheres and the Empyrean above, which, according to Maimonides, is exactly 112,420,000 kilometers from earth. (That is, a man walking forty kilometers a day on a level road at 2000 paces per kilometer, 365 days a year, would theoretically reach the Empyrean in 7700 years. Jesus, however, ascended in an instant.) The angels are arranged in three hierarchies of three orders each. The highest, and closest to God, are the seraphim, cherubim, and thrones. Below them are the dominions, virtues, and powers. At the lowest rank are the principalities, archangels, and the angels simply called "angels."

Angelic seraphim appear only once in the Bible. (Elsewhere in the Old Testament, seraphim are snakes, natural and supernatural.) Isaiah sees them when he ascends to heaven in a vision. They have six wings: two cover their face, two cover their feet, and with two they fly. They cry: "Holy, holy, holy, is the Lord of hosts: the whole earth is full of his glory." Their voices rock the doorposts and the "temple" or "house" of God fills with smoke. Gregory of Nyssa said that Lucifer was originally a seraph and had twelve wings, but most doubted this. Alan of Lille in the 12th century said they "are fiery, mobile, keen-sighted, discriminating, delicate, illuminated by an unmediated fountain of lights. . . They glow with great love for the divine." In later iconography, the seraphim's cries of celebration turn into song and they become the hosts of angels singing and playing musical instruments from the ceilings and corners of churches.

A seraph puts a burning coal on Isaiah's lips and he is purified. This would become controversial: Early Christians such as Origen considered Jesus to be a kind of angel, and that this seraph was Jesus himself. Later Christians denied it: In the words of Hugh of St. Victor in the 12th century, the seraph was merely "an exemplar of the total person of Christ." Since the seraph was not Jesus, they then wondered: Was the angel acting

PANDESALUTAREMDOMINOUINCENTETRIUMPHUM
LINGUAFIGURAMANUSLABIUMUOXSYLLABASENS?
MAGNACRUCISDOMINIQUEMGLORIAPOSCITUBIG;
SIDERACELSASUPERETQUOPERTINGITABYSSUS
LUXUBIPURAMANETQUOTETRASILENTIANOCTIS
PERPETUAELATITANTUBINOXQDIESQUICISSIM
SUCCEDUNTCEDUNTQSIBIQUOTEMPORECUNCTUS
LABITURORBISUBIUARIABILISINDITORDOEST
QUATTUORISTOUINCIREUIXSUFFICITASTHAEC
PAGINADIGNACRUCIPRAECONIATRAMITEDENAS
HASQUEQUADRAGENASSANCTODECALLEMONADES
ARTELIGARESIMULPLENASQUOQUELUCESERENA
MYSTICAGASUIRTUSORNATCONSECRATHONORAT
TEMPORISINSTANTISDUMERUSHICRITEFIGURA
GESTATQUOTOTACHRISTOSUBPRINCIPESANCTA
ECCLESIARABIDOPIGFERTCONTRARIATEABIC
OBPONENSHOSTIBELLATRIXCONSCIAPERSTANS
UIRTUTUMETPUCHISUITIASIBILAUSEACUNCTA
CUMFIDEISCUTODOMATHAECRITUHASTAQUERBO
LORICALIGATETBENEIUSTITIAEINTUITALMAM
ATQSALUTARISGALEAMHANCINGERTICEGESTAT
IPSACRUCISCLARAFACIUNTINSICNIAFRONTEM
FRONTISETADUERSAEFUNDUNTFORMOSADECORE
INCRUCESALUATORSAEUUMNAQUICERATHOSTEM
EIUSETHOCNUMEROSUADESERTOALMATRAHEBAT
EXDAPIBUSCUNCTISIEIUNIASOBRIACHRISTUS
STRINXERATERIPUITQEARTODEFAUCESUPERBI
RAPTORISHOMINEMQUEMCASTRIMARGIATRAXIT
INFACINUSDIRUMINMITEMSIMULATTULITIRAM
HUICEFHILARGIRIALEUISETCENODOXIATRUSIT
QUEMAREGNODOMINUSAETERNAREDEMTIOIESUS
SEDPRESSITHOSTEMPRAEDAMSALUAUITABYPSO
DAPSILISATQEHUMILISMITISETSOBRIUSIPSE
CUIUSPUGNASALUSCUIUSUICTORIASANCTAEST
CUIUSINARCETHRONUSASPECTININFIMACUIVS
CRUXOUATORBISHONORCRUXESTERECTIOMUNDI
CRUXMIHICARMENERITCRISTIUICTORIACLARA

on his own or by command of God? Can one become instantly purified from without—even by an angel in heaven—rather than slowly purified from within by penance and prayer?

According to her hagiographer, when Catherine of Siena married Jesus, a seraph gave her a ring inlaid with stones that only she could see, and that were brighter or duller according to her good deeds. (According to Catherine herself, Jesus indeed gave her an invisible ring, but it was made from his own foreskin.) Francis of Assisi in the 13th century received the stigmata from a seraph, who was somehow in the form of the crucified Christ. Many of his followers, including Ignatius Loyola in the 16th century, believed that Francis himself was an angel, "alembicated into the human viscera"—specifically the sixth of the seven angels of the Apocalypse, the one who dries up the river Euphrates, though it is not known why this specific angel was selected.

In the Bible, the cherubim, who are Mesopotamian holdovers, are not angels. There are only two of them. In the Empyrean, Yahweh dwells between them, and when he travels to earth, they are the storm winds that carry him on his throne, or carry him without his throne. According to the *Songs of the Sabbath Sacrifice*, found among the Dead Sea Scrolls, the cumulative effect of their "tumult of jubilation"—the flapping wings, the songs of praise—is "the sound of divine stillness." One of them was temporarily posted along with a rotating, flaming sword at the gates of Eden to keep Adam and Eve from returning. Ezekiel says that each has four wings and four faces—that of a man, an ox, a lion, and an eagle— with human hands and the hooves of a calf the color of burnished brass. Later, Ezekiel says again that each has four faces, but this time that of a man, a lion, an eagle, and, mysteriously, a cherub. Even later he says that each has two faces. (The commentators would explain that he must have been looking at them in profile.) Strangely, the cherub that Ezekiel meets gives him a scroll, written with "lamentations and mourning and woe," and commands him to eat it; it tastes like honey.

In other places in the Bible the cherubim have only one face and one pair of wings, but four feet. In Revelation, they are called "animals," not cherubim, and there are four, not two—a man, an ox, a lion, and an eagle—with only one face each, six wings, and eyes "all around as well as inside," which is difficult to visualize. Nevertheless, cherubim were in some manner portrayed on the Ark of the Covenant, and Solomon's elaborate temple was carved and gilded with figures of cherubim and palm trees and flowers. It is only much later in Christianity that they are elevated to the status of angels and become chubby boys or babies with wings.

Aquinas proved that Gregory of Nyssa was incorrect, and that the fall of the rebel angels began with a cherub, not a seraph:

> "Cherubim" is interpreted "fullness of knowledge," while "Seraphim" means "those who are on fire," or "who set on fire." Consequently Cherubim is derived from knowledge; which is compatible with mortal sin; but Seraphim is derived from the heat of charity, which is incompatible with mortal sin. Therefore the first angel who sinned is called, not a Seraph, but a Cherub.

The cherubim, said Richard of St. Victor in the 12th century, lead the soul into "secret places of divine incomprehensibility," the knowledge that is beyond human reasoning. It was either a cherub or a seraph who pierced the heart of Teresa of Ávila in 1559 with a burning sword:

> I saw an angel appear in bodily form close by my left side. . . He was not large, but small, and extremely beautiful. His face was aflame with fire so much that he appeared to be one of the highest ranks of angels, those that we call seraphim or cherubim. Their names, angels never tell me, but I'm well aware that in heaven there are great differences between different types of angels, though I can't explain it.
>
> In his hands, I saw a golden spear, with an iron tip at the end that appeared to be on fire. He plunged it into my heart several times, all the way to my entrails. When he drew it out,

he seemed to draw them out, as well, leaving me all on fire with love for God.

The pain was so strong that it made me moan several times, and yet the sweetness of the pain was so surpassing that I couldn't possibly wish to be rid of it. . . This pain lasted many days, and during that time, I didn't want to see or speak to anyone, but only to cherish my pain, which gave me a greater bliss than any created things could give me.

The thrones, dominions, virtues, powers, and principalities are not specifically mentioned as angels in the Bible. Their origin seems to derive from passages that may refer to the general concepts and not their specific angelization. For example, in Colossians, all things were created by God, "whether they be thrones or dominions, or principalities, or powers." Or in Peter: "For I am persuaded that neither death nor life, nor angels, nor principalities, nor powers, nor things present, nor things to come. . . shall be able to separate us from the love of God." (That is, the cult of angels, as Paul had warned, is an obstacle or a distraction to the worship of God.) Augustine confessed he had no idea who these angels are or what they do.

Hadewijch in the 13th century was taken to paradise by a throne, who explained to her the meanings of various allegorical trees growing there and then introduced her to Jesus. Bonaventure claimed to have spoken to one of the virtues, and early on it was believed by some that the virtues move the heavenly spheres. This was decisively disproved by Isaac Newton, who nevertheless believed the spheres were protected from harmful comets by an angelic shield. (With the European discovery of the New World, it was speculated that after the Flood angels had transported people to the far-flung corners of the earth, but it was not said which order of angels had been given the task or how exactly it was accomplished.)

According to Gregory the Great, the angels deliver ordinary messages and the archangels deliver the most important messages, such as the

Annunciation to Mary. (Though one wonders what a routine message from God would be.) Only a few of the archangels are given individual names and it is uncertain which of the named archangels are actually archangels. The word only appears twice in the Bible, once generically and once referring only to Michael, seen by Daniel in a vision as the protector of Israel. In Revelation, Michael (not identified as an archangel) leads the army of angels that defeats Satan, who is in the form of a dragon. Bonaventure said he was a prince of the seraphim, Aquinas that he was a prince of the angels called "angels."

Moreover, Michael is an angel who is somehow also a saint, without having been human. As the warrior from Revelation, he became the patron of medieval knights, the defender of the faith, and the one who told Joan of Arc in the 15th century to take up arms. In a 17th century fresco by Domenichino in Naples, he stomps on the heretics Luther and Calvin. Michael heals the sick. He carries the dead to heaven—a journey that was also transformed into a symbolic crossing of the Jordan River ("Michael row the boat ashore"). In heaven, he weighs the good deeds of the soul, while the devil tries to tip the balance. From the 4th century on, his shrines have been built across Christendom, usually on high and rocky places; from the 6th century on, his Feast Day, Michaelmas, has been an important event on the calendar. He is invoked in the Catholic rite for exorcism (where, oddly, the "principalities and powers" are forces of evil). Early Protestants and later groups such as the Seventh-Day Adventists and the Jehovah's Witnesses have maintained that he is identical to Christ—that is, he is the non-incarnate Christ, the one before and after Jesus' time on earth. The Mormons believe that Michael was Adam. Rudolf Steiner said that the current era, the Age of Michael, began on the astral plane in late November, 1879, with the triumph of light over darkness, coincidentally the time when the teenaged Steiner moved from the village of Neudörfl to Vienna.

Robert Bellarmine in the 17th century said that every kingdom has two kings, a visible man and an invisible angel; every church has two bishops, a man and an angel; and the Church has two popes, the visible pope and the Archangel Michael.

The Catholic Church also recognizes Raphael and Gabriel as archangels. Raphael, traditionally healer of the sick and protector of travelers, is not named in the Bible. He is a major character in the sometimes apocryphal Book of Tobit: He cures Tobit, who became blind when the droppings of sparrows fell in his eyes, and he arranges the marriage of Tobit's son Tobias to his cousin Sarah, whose seven previous husbands had all died on their wedding night. (He instructs the couple to avoid the curse by burning the heart and liver of a miraculous fish in their nuptial chamber.) In the apocryphal Book of Enoch, Raphael throws the fallen angel Azazel alive into a pit and covers it with rocks, for Azazel had taught men how to make weapons of war and women how to dye their hair and paint their eyebrows. It was said that Raphael healed the circumcision of Abraham, who had neglected to have it done until late in life.

Legend has it that before the Flood, Raphael gave Noah the *Book of the Angel Raziel*, to teach him how to construct the ark. This book contains all celestial and earthly knowledge, the laws of nature and of the stars, the power of language and the force of each letter of the alphabet. (And perhaps more: the *Zohar* says that in the middle of the book is secret writing with the 1500 keys to the mystery of the universe, "which were not revealed even to the holy angels.") The book, first given by the angel Raziel to Adam, was hidden then recovered repeatedly over the centuries, and was the source of the wisdom of Abraham, Moses, Enoch, and Solomon. The book still exists, though the present version was possibly written by Eleazar of Worms in the 13th century.

Gabriel makes only three appearances in the Bible, foretelling the births of John the Baptist and of Jesus, and interpreting Daniel's visions ("The hairy he-goat is the king of Javan. . ."). He does not have a trumpet, contrary to Milton and African-American spirituals, though he may be one of the unnamed angels of the Apocalypse, who do. In Islam, where he is Jibril, he has 140 pairs of wings and dictated the Qur'an to Mohammed. Ficino thought that the star that guided the Magi to Bethlehem was actually Gabriel in the form of a comet, making visible the angels' "invisible light of understanding" by compressing it into dense air. The Mormons believe that Gabriel, who was not an archangel, was Noah.

In 826, a blind man named Alberic, sleeping in the church of St. Marcellinus in Seligenstadt, saw an old man dressed in white. The man asked Alberic if he knew who he was and Alberic replied, "St. Marcellinus." The vision told him that he was Gabriel, taking on the "person and form" of Marcellinus. He had come to say that he approved the recent controversial translation of the saint's relics to Seligenstadt by Einhard, Charlemagne's secretary. This was an important event. It resolved the question of how the saints were frequently appearing everywhere, sometimes even in armor, when the dead will not assume their bodies again until the Last Judgment, as well as Augustine's belief that the dead do not concern themselves with the affairs of the living. The apparitions of saints, giving counsel or intervening in local matters, were actually angels disguised as the saints.

The fourth named angel is Uriel, who is frequent in the apocryphal books—and in the poetry of H. D. in the 20th century—but is not in the Bible. He is sometimes an archangel, sometimes a seraph, sometimes the cherub who guards Eden, sometimes the Angel of Death in the seven plagues of Egypt, sometimes the angel who wrestled with Jacob, sometimes the messenger who warned Noah of the coming flood, sometimes the angel who excoriated Moses for neglecting to circumcise his son Gershom or the angel who rescued John the Baptist from Herod's massacre of the innocents, sometimes a pitiless exacter of repentance, sometimes the one who taught humankind Kabbalah and the art of alchemy. Milton called him "the sharpest-sighted spirit in all of Heaven." He is the only angel given to theological monologues, though it is unclear whether he is speaking or God is speaking through him. In 2 Esdras (also known as 4 Esdras) he engages the prophet Ezra in long paradoxical discussions on the unknowability of God. He tells Ezra of the coming end of the world, when the sun will shine at night and the moon by day, when stars will fall out of the sky, when fires will break out and wild beasts roam freely, when sweet water will turn salty, when blood will drip from wood and stones will speak, when the birds will fly off and not return, when the nations will realize that not a single righteous person has passed among them, and when "one shall reign whom those who dwell on earth do not expect," who will "make his voice heard by night and all shall hear his voice."

Later, Ezra hears the voice of God himself, who commands him to fast for forty days, and then gather a heap of blank tablets and five scribes "trained to write rapidly." Ezra is given a cup of liquid to drink, "something like water, but its color was like fire." He begins to speak, and the five scribes write "what was dictated, in characters which they did not know." He speaks and they write for forty days; they produce ninety-four books. God tells Ezra that the "worthy and unworthy" may read the first twenty-four, but that the remaining seventy may only be shown to the "wise among your people." God says that "in them is the spring of understanding, the fountain of wisdom, and the river of knowledge." The fate of these books is unknown.

In Revelation, there are seven angels with seven trumpets, and a tradition that waxed and waned added three archangels to the usual four. Gregory the Great named them as Simiel, Oriphiel, and Raguel. The Byzantine Church had Selaphiel (Salathiel), Jegudiel (Jehudiel), and Barachiel—but sometimes included a fourth, Jerahmeel (Jeremiel). The Copts removed Uriel and added Suriel, Zadkiel, Sarathiel, and Aniel. The apocryphal Book of Enoch had Raguel, Sariel, and Jerahmeel. Other apocryphal books named Izidkiel, Hanael, and Kepharel. The seven angels corresponded to the seven days of the week and to the seven visible planetary bodies (sun, moon, Mercury, Venus, Mars, Jupiter, Saturn), with angels often being assigned to each, though not consistently.

The confusion was alleviated in the Catholic Church for more than a century in 1460, when Gabriel appeared to the Franciscan monk, Johannes Menesius de Silva, known as Amadeus of Portugal, in a cave outside of Rome. Gabriel dictated a book to Amadeus, the *Apocalipsis Nova*, where the three other archangels were revealed to be Barachiel, Sealtiel, and Jehudiel. Gabriel also told Amadeus that in the near future, the last emperor would reunite the world in one faith, presided over by an angelic pope, and history would come to an end. The archangel had instructed Amadeus to seal the book, which could not be opened until the last days, but somehow its contents circulated. In Rome, a church was built over the baths of Diocletian, Santa Maria degli Angeli, designed by Michelangelo, to honor the new covenant. The Hapsburg monarchs declared that the seven angels would be the holy custodians of their dominions, and they became frequent in the iconography and devotions of the New World. Veneration of the Seven continued there long after they were suppressed in Europe on the grounds that the non-canonical angels may well be disguised demons.

Above all, the celestial hierarchy served as a taxonomy of the emblems of a devout life. Among many examples, Bernard of Clairvaux writes:

> God in the Seraphim loves as Charity, in the Cherubim He knows as Truth, in the Thrones He presides as Justice, in the Dominions He reigns as Majesty, in the Principalities He rules as Law, in the Powers He defends as Salvation, in the Virtues He acts as Might, in the Archangels He reveals as Light, in the Angels He comforts as Kindness.

Or Bonaventure:

> Note that on the first level, truth is to be invoked by sighs and prayer, which pertains to the Angels; it is to be received by studying and reading, which pertains to the Archangels; it is to be communicated by example and preaching, which pertains to the Principalities.
>
> On the second level, truth is to be sought by recourse and dedication to it, which pertains to the Powers; it is to be grasped by activity and endeavor, which pertains to the Virtues; it is to be assimilated by self-contempt and mortification, which pertains to the Dominions.

On the third level, truth is to be adored by sacrifice and praise, which pertains to the Thrones; it is to be admired in ecstasy and contemplation, which pertains to the Cherubim; it is to be embraced with caresses and love, which pertains to the Seraphim.

Note these things carefully, for they hold the fountain of life.

```
D I G N A M O P U S E T C L A R A M U I C T O R I S P S A L L E R E R E G I S
U E X I L L U M I N S I G N E D O M I N A N T I S L A U D E T R I U m p h u m
Q U O M U N D U M E R I P U I T N O Q U G O E T S C E P T R A T Y R A N N I
D I S S T R U X I T R E P R O B A C T O R I S R E G M I N A F A L S A
Q U O B E N E S U S T E N T A T C A E L U M P Y L A G U S Q U E S O L U M Q E
C U I U S I N O R B E S A C R A E X F U E R I T T N A A L T A T I O Q U A N D O
M Y S T E R I O A D C U R R E N S N A S C E N T I S A B O R I G I M U N D I
A N N O R U M S A E C L I S E R I E S H A E C A T T U L I T A T Q U E H I N C
I U R E S A C R A E F I D E I P L E B E S C O N C U R R E R E S C R I P T I S
C R E D E N T E S F E C I T P R O B A C O N D I T O R O M N I A C O N D E N S
T E M P O R A C U M N U M E R O C O N C O R D A N S C U N C T A S A C R A T O
C U N C T A Q U I A D O M I N U S R E N O V A V I T S A E C U L A P R I S C A
S A N G U I N E A M R E C R E A N S P E R F E C I T C U N C T A C R U O R E
I A M B O D U S I N P R I M I S T U N F I N X I T Q U A E E X A D I E B U S
P R I N C I P I U T G E N E S I S P I E S A N C T O D O G M A T E P A N D I T
S I C Q U E D I E S E X T A H O M I N E M R E P A R A N D O R E D E M P T O R
S A B B A T A D E M O N S T R A N S C E L E B R A V I T S A B B A T A V E R E
E T P R A T H A N C N U M E R U S U S S U M Q U O P A S S I O F A L S O
L A T I N O C P R E M A T T E M P T A N T E H A N C S I A A T I
O T E M B A T C U R A R U M U L N C T A S T P A R S S I A D I R M
Q U O D N U M Q U A M P O S T H A E C F A L L A C I S F A C T I O P L E B I S
I A M O S T E N T E T P A N D A T P I E T A T I S S E D P R O B A U I R T U S
D O G M A T A U E R A D E I P E R C U R I T A H A E C T E M P O R A M U N D I
S A N C T I F I C A R E C R U C E M B E N E D I C E R E R E N G A F U T U R A
Q U A E E S S E T S A L U A T O R B E N E D I C T A P O T E N T I A P A T R I S
N E M P E D A T U R U S E I S S U M M O N O V A P R O E M I A C H R I S T U S
Q U O S M O N I T I S F L E X I T D O C U I T Q U O S U E R B A S A L U T I S
A T C R U C I S H A E C S P E C I E S T R I B U I T S O L A M I N A F I D I S
M A T E R I A M L A U D I S B O N I T A T E H I N C S C I R E C R E A N T I S
Q U I P I U S O M N I P O T E N S U I T A M E D I T A N T E S A L U B R E M
Q U A N D O H O M I N E M U O L U I T P A R A D T S U M S O R T E T E N E R E
E T P O S T L A P S A F U G A M M I S E R A N S Q U O G N O L U I T I P S U M
F R A U D E P E R I R E R E L U P I H A N C A X I M E C O N D I T O R A R C E M
S E D C R U C I S A D U I T A M U D I C A U E R A T O R B I H U I C
U I R T U T U U T N U M E R O G U E G E T A D S C E P T R A S U P E R N A
S P E S A M O R A T Q U E F I D E S O M N E S Q U O S S A N X I T A B A E G O
P E R P E T U O D I G N O S C H R I S T I U E N E R A B I L E U I S U B H I N C
```

4.

The angelic order was primarily revealed by Dionysius the Areopagite in his book *The Celestial Hierarchy*. (He invented the word "hierarchy.") Dionysius is mentioned in one sentence in Acts: Paul arrives in Athens, finds it "full of idols," and goes to the market to argue with Stoic and Epicurean philosophers. He is brought before the Areopagus—named after the place, the Hill of Ares/Mars, where it is located—a judicial council that originally or mythologically heard contentions between the gods and now deals with more civic matters. Paul notes that the Athenians have an altar to an "unknown god," erected as protection against a possible powerful foreign god of which they presently are unaware. That god, Paul says, is the One True God, whom the Greeks once worshiped long ago, before they descended into idolatry. He is mocked by all, but one of the members of the court, Dionysius, and a "woman named Damaris" stand by him. According to Eusebius of Caesarea in the 4th century—citing the otherwise unknown Dionysius of Corinth—Dionysius the Areopagite then became the first bishop of Athens. Hilduin, Bishop of Paris in the 9th century, said that Dionysius was none other than France's venerated St. Denis.

Jacobus de Voragine's authoritative 13th century book on the saints, *The Golden Legend*—second only to the Bible in popularity in the late European Middle Ages—tells the story at greater length. After much debate, Dionysius challenges Paul to make a blind man see. The miracle performed, he and his wife Damaris convert. Dionysius studies with Paul for three years, and learns from him about the hierarchy of the angels, for Paul, as surprisingly only briefly mentioned in 2 Corinthians, had been taken to the highest heaven. He becomes bishop of Athens, and converts the whole city. Pope Clement sends him to Paris to preach to the heathens of Gaul, where Dionysius (now known as Denis) builds churches, installs clerics, and brings the Gospel to many.

Satan provokes the emperor Domitian against the Christians. Denis is arrested and beaten, but refuses to recant. He is stretched on an iron grill over a fire, but he sings from the Psalms, "Thy word is refined by fire and thy servant has loved it," and the fire doesn't harm him. He is put in a cage with hungry wild beasts, but he makes the sign of the cross over them and the beasts become tame. He is thrown into an oven but the fire goes out. They nail him to a cross but he lives. He is sent back to prison where he celebrates the mass and Jesus himself appears in a brilliant light. Finally, he is beheaded before a statue of Mercury. Denis stands up, takes his head in his hands and walks for two miles from the place called Montmartre, the hill of martyrs, to the resting place he has chosen.

Almost seven hundred years later, an ambassador of Emperor Michael the Stammerer of Constantinople brings a copy of *The Celestial Hierarchy* to King Louis, son of Charlemagne, and nineteen fatally ill people are instantly cured at the mere sight of the book. Some centuries before, de Voragine writes, "King Clovis irreverently uncovered the body of St. Denis, broke off an arm bone, and took it away. In no time he lost his mind."

The author of *The Celestial Hierarchy* and other important works attributed to him was translated by various luminaries, including John Scotus Eriugena in the 9th century, Robert Grosseteste in the 13th century, and the anonymous author of *The Cloud of Unknowing* in the 14th century; was influential on such divines as Meister Eckhart, Jan van Ruusbroec, and Julian of Norwich in the 14th century, Nicholas of Cusa in the 15th century, John of the Cross and Teresa of Ávila in the 16th century, among many others; and was quoted, to take one example, by Aquinas at least 1700 times. The author claimed to be the Biblical Dionysius the Areopagite, and had both witnessed the dormition of Mary (a scene unmentioned in the Bible) and comforted John in exile on Patmos, but doubts were expressed as early as 532 by Hypatius of Ephesus. Hypatius argued that if the texts were indeed authentic, they surely would have been known previously to the Blessed Cyril of Alexandria in the 5th century, but he does not cite them.

Because of various indications, including concepts and phrases taken from the Neo-Platonist philosopher Proclus, who died in 485, it is now believed that the texts were written in Syria sometime in the late 5th or early 6th century—and that St. Denis of Paris was yet another, third person. Since 1895, the author has been universally known as Pseudo-

Dionysius the Areopagite. He has been variously identified as Ammonius Saccas in the 3rd century (who may have been two people and who may have come from India), Sergius of Reshaina in the 6th century, Peter the Fuller or Peter the Iberian in the 5th century, Dionysius the Great in the 3rd century, and Dionysius the Scholastic of Gaza (who may be Dorotheus of Gaza) in the 6th century, among others. The most ingenious theory was presented in 1928 by the German scholar Joseph Stiglmayr. He claimed that the author was the monophysite Severus the Great of Antioch in the 6th century, on the grounds that Severus was the only person of such intelligence alive at that time in that place.

Besides *The Celestial Hierarchy*, Pseudo-Dionysius is now known as the author of two other books (*The Divine Names* and *The Ecclesiastical Hierarchy*); an enigmatic essay, "The Mystical Theology," that elucidates the apophatic method (God is beyond anything we could know or imagine about him); and ten letters, of which five are of disputed origin. In his writings, Pseudo-Dionysius also refers to seven of his other books—*Theological Representations, Symbolic Theology, On Angelic Properties and Orders, On the Just and Divine Judgement, On Intelligible and Sensible Beings, On the Divine Hymns, and On the Soul*—but these are all believed to be not lost but entirely fictitious.

Many argued over whether the hierarchies were properly named and in the correct ascending order. Even Aquinas admitted: "Our knowledge of the angels is imperfect, as Dionysius says. Hence we can only distinguish the angelic offices and orders in a general way, so as to place many angels in one order. But if we knew the offices and distinctions of the angels perfectly, we should know perfectly that each angel has his own office and his own order among things, and much more so than any star, though this be hidden from us."

Martin Luther was more adamant:

Dionysisus, whoever he may have been. . . shows hardly any signs of solid learning. I would ask, by what authority and with what arguments does he prove his hodge-podge about the angels in his *Celestial Hierarchy*—a book over which many curious and superstitious spirits have cudgeled their brains? If one were to read and judge without prejudice, is not everything in it his own fancy and very much like a dream?

The dream reappeared in Duino Castle in January, 1912, as recorded by Princess Marie von Thurn und Taxis:

Rilke climbed down to the bastions which, jutting to the east and west, were connected to the foot of the castle by a narrow path along the cliffs. These cliffs fall steeply, for about two hundred feet, into the sea. Rilke paced back and forth, deep in thought. . . . Then, all at once, in the midst of his brooding, he halted suddenly, for it seemed to him that in the raging of the storm a voice had called to him: "Who, if I cried out, would hear me among the angelic orders?" (*Wer, wenn ich schriee, hörte mich denn aus der Engel Ordnungen?*)…

```
CRUXMIHICARMENERITAURESADIBETEFIDELES
LAUSCRUCISOREMANATDEUOTASDUCITEMENTES
UOSQUIB;ESTCRISTUSQUIB;ESTSAPIENTIACURAE
LUXAETERNADEIQUIBUSINCORRUPTIOAMORFIT
HICSONATARTIFICISUIRTUSOPERISQUEBEATI
HICDECOREXULTATHICGLORIAFINGITURARTIS
UESTERHONORUIUITQUIAUIUIDAFULGETORIGO
UESTRAMANETPALMAUREINMORTALISINAETRA
CLARAQUIAESTUOBISUICTORIACRISTUSUBIQVE
IPSESALUSUESTRAEQUINDICTAMFECITINATRO
PROUOBISMORIENSIUSTEQEOBPRESSITINIQUM
MORTEINTERFICIENSMORTEMDUTARTARAUICIT
HUCHUCAEGROTIUOLUCRICONCURRITECURSUEN
UESTERERITMEDIC;QEMCRUXMEDICABILISALTO
STIPITEGESTAUITEXTENDITBRACHIACURAEET
POSCITECURARIETGEMINASEXPANDITEPALMAS
IPSIUSERGOUALETTACTUCITOINHORAEADEM
REDDEREDESTRAPIATREPIDOHICALMAQIETIS
SUMMACUESTUIRTUSSAPIENSADIBERESALUTE
ARSQUIDESCENDITRESIPISCATFISICAUTARTE
DAMPNATIMORISEANTREDIUIUANTISGNABEATA
QUINQUASALUTAREMNUMERUMHICGINTABEATAE
DATCRUCISHAECSPECIESDIUINOMUNEREPLENA
QUISIGNATUENIAMQUISABBATALAETAQUIETIS
QUILEGISPRISCAEPOSTAZIMAFESTATRIBUTAE
ESTINDEXETPOSTSANCTASOLLEMPNIAPASCHAE
IPSEPARACLETIMISSIUNDIQUENUMINEPLENUS
PACISAMOREPROBUSPACISSIGNACULAPROFERT
PERFECTUSDECORESPECIEPERFECTUSHONORIS
QUINGECRUCESPRAEBETRAMISDENASQ;MONADES
XNUMERATSEMPERQ;CRUCIAPTAETAMICAFIGURA
QUINQUELIBRILEGISEXTANTMANDATAQUEDENA
OMNIANEMPECRUCICONCORDANTTRAMITEDICTU
LEXNUMERUSTEMPUSMYSTERIAFACTACARACTER
OMNESERGOCRUCEMPARITERLAUDEMUSOUANTES
SOLUAMUSUOTAHINCCRUCIFIXOETDEBITAREGI
SANGUINEQUIPROPRIOLAXAUITCRIMINAMUNDO
```

5.

Angels hovering all round:

Iahhel,
the angel of philosophers and recluses;

                              Heiglot,
                              the angel of snowstorms;

Melchisedec,
who fed the animals on Noah's ark;

                    Memuneh,
                    the dispenser of dreams;

                              Kerubiel,
                              whose body is full of burning coals;

Jalula,
who carries the cup of oblivion,
so that a soul can drink
and forget all that it has known;

                         Sadriel,
                         the angel of order;

                                   Teiazel,
                                   guardian of librarians;

Nadiel,
the angel of migration;

                    Maktiel,
                    who rules over trees;

> *Halqim,*
> who guards the gate of the North Wind;

Poteh,
the angel of forgetting;

> *Semanglaf,*
> who helps the pregnant;

> > *Purson,*
> > who knows the past and future,
> > who rides a bear, who carries a viper
> > in his hand and has the face of a lion;

Kafziel,
who governs the death of kings;

> *Nuriel,*
> the angel of hailstorms;

> > *Matarel,*
> > the angel of rain;

Mach,
who can make you invisible;

> *Nahaliel,*
> who rules the running streams;

Shetel and *Anush* and *Aebel,*
who roasted meat for Adam
and cooled his wine;

Shemael,
who stands at the window of heaven to listen
to the songs of praise rising from the houses below;

Hanum,
the angel of Monday;

Taliahad,
the angel of water;

Pravuil,
the smartest of the archangels,
who keeps the heavenly books and records;

Ihaniel,
who protects fruit-bearing trees;

Machidiel,
who can bring a man the maiden of his desire;

Naoutha,
with a rod of snow he puts in his
mouth to quench the fire within;

Jehudiam,
who carries the seventy keys
to the treasures of the Lord;

Shateiel,
the angel of silence;

Rashiel,
the angel of whirlwinds and earthquakes;

Samael,
the angel of death,
who seduced Eve and was the father of Cain;

> *Isaac,*
> who was not the human son of Abraham,
> but an angel of light;

Damabiah,
who watches over shipbuilding;

> *Schrewniel,*
> who can bestow a good memory;

Penemue,
who taught mankind the corrupting art of writing;

> *Hakamiah,*
> guardian angel of France;

Riddia,
angel of rain, who takes the form
of a young heifer with cleft lips;

> *Trsiel,*
> angel of the rivers;

> > *Ouestucati,*
> > who brings the sea winds;

Ashmadai,
who got Noah drunk and who slew
the seven bridegrooms of Sarah;

Nathanael,
who guards hidden things;

Zagzagel,
who speaks the seventy languages;

Hemah,
who determines the death of domestic animals;

Tabris,
the angel of free will;

Amarlia,
who cures boils;

Harbonah,
the donkey driver, an angel of confusion;

Hashmal,
who speaks in fire and who incinerated
a student reading the Book of Ezekiel
and no one knew why;

Iophiel,
who drove Adam and Eve out of Eden;

Pahardon,
the angel of terror;

Gagiel,
who has dominion over fish;

Dumah,
the angel of dreams and silence;

Yasriel,
keeper of the seventy holy pencils
for inscribing the name of the Lord;

        Tubiel,
        who returns small birds to their owners;

Zalbesael,
the angel of the rainy season;

        Alphun,
        the angel of doves;

        Trgiaob,
        who watches over creeping things;

Harahel,
the angel in charge of archives and libraries;

        Anabiel and *Hodniel* and *Kabniel,*
        who can cure stupidity;

Azariel,
who can cure stupidity and
who helps the fishermen catch large fish;

        Naamah,
        the angel of prostitution;

Paraqlitos,
guardian angel of the sorrows of death;

        Raamiel,
        the angel of thunder;

Achaiah,
the angel of patience;

Anauel,
who protects bankers and brokers;

Ararita,
who protects against sudden death;

Zikiel,
the angel of comets;

Balberith,
who notarizes pacts made with the devil;

Bardiel,
the angel of hail;

Caim,
a fallen angel in the form of a thrush;

Camael,
who appears as a leopard crouched on a rock;

Temeluch,
who cares for babies born from adultery;

John the Baptist,
who was not a man but an angel;

Asmoday,
who teaches mathematics
and can make men invisible;

Shakziel,
who rules the insects that live on the water;

Forneus,
who causes men to be loved by their enemies;

El El,
who also guards the gates of the North Wind;

Causub,
who can charm snakes;

Radueriel,
the angel of poetry;

Sandalphon,
whom Moses met, with his 70,000 heads;

Dumah,
the angel of silence and the stillness of death;

Cetarari,
the angel of winter;

Hahaiah,
who reveals mysteries to mortals;

The Angel of Clouds,
who has no other name;

Rampel,
the angel of mountains;

Silmai,
angel of the River Jordan;

63

Anael,
angel of the Star of Love;

> *Umahel,*
> whose mission is unknown;

Salamiel,
one of the Watchers,
taller than a giant and eternally silent;

> *Gazardiel,*
> who oversees the rising and the setting of the sun;

Charbiel,
who dried the waters after the Flood;

> *Israfel,*
> who will blow his horn on Judgment Day and
> then die in the great fire at the end of the world;

Azrael,
who is forever writing in a huge book and forever erasing what he wrote:
the names of the born and the names of the dead.

Birgitta of Sweden said:
"If we saw an angel clearly, we should die of pleasure."

6.

1898: In a small unpainted wood church in a clearing on the Fraser River, they sing:

Awsthawm ta ay-e See-am,
       Maytla, maytla;
Owa-tchuh kukh ta skwi-la-wal,
       Maytla, maytla;
O! hayluk skwi-la-wal,
       A-yelokh whulam tokla lee-awm,
Lay, ska talowa See-am,
Owe-awts hayluk.

                    (There is a happy land,
                            Far, far away;
                    Where the bright angels stand,
                            Bright, bright as day.
                    There, we will always sing,
                            Glory to our Savior, King,
                    Loud let his praises ring,
                            Praise, praise for aye.)

65

They sing:

Tchalal telth-le-melth `kup lay ta
Stawlos ta Tchee-tchilth-See-am,
Whaw-ay-e-im ta kas ta tchee-tchilth stawla,
Ta shwalays ta ay-e lee-zas.

Tchalal telthlemelth `kup lay ta stawlo,
Ta ay-e, osthayte ay-e stawlo. . .

> (Shall we gather at the river,
> Where bright angel-feet have trod;
> With its crystal tide forever
> Flowing by the throne of God.
>
> Yes, we'll gather at the river,
> The beautiful, the beautiful river. . .)

7.

In most cultures a corpse is laid on its back, and gravity pulls the fluids down, giving the upper sections their waxy pallor. The lower sections darken as the blood settles, except in those places where the body is touching the surface on which it is laid. There, the pressure of the weight of the corpse pushes the blood from the tissue, forming areas that are much lighter than the rest. One of those areas is across the shoulder blades and upper back, and it takes the form of perfectly symmetrical wings. The Cathars believed that humans are fallen angels, trapped in a material body because of the sin of the rebellion.

ARBORODORÆPOTENSFRONDOSOQUERTICELATA
QUASUMMAUEREṢACROUELUITORDINEᵛBERTAS
ORTUSDITATUSETPARCUINULLUSINORBEEST
FLORIBUSETFOLIISMILLENOGERMINEDIUES
OMNESEXCEDENSALTASCRAUITUDINESILUAS
CUMTOTAMPIEMAGNUSUESTITHONOSQDECUSQ
AMBITUERUSHONORLAETUSLOQUITUREAUOTO
STANSHOMOLIUORHOCNATIONIDENEGATATRI
DEMONISHORRENDUSREMSCIRILAUDEMOUERI
ARBORSOLATENENSUARIOSUIRTUTECOLORES
PURPUREOREGISSUBTACTUROSCIDAFULGENS
AETERNOESRADIOSTANTINTENAMPIQUINCTE
ÆDESTURRITÆEXHOCDUDUMESTNONNEBEATA
MACHINÆTIPSADEIARÆTQUIUSITSUPREMA
LARHOCNEESTETMIRALUCERNAHOCOTIATOTA
AÇN;HOCSTATUITSIGNANSQUOQUERITEUIANDO
UERASALUSISTAQUODUERUSFONSBONITATIS
ESTBENEDICTIOQ:SACRAUITAMORPIETASQUE
SANCTASALUTISLUXETUITAREDEMPTIOUERA
INQ:DOMUPRINCEPSDONUMDATPACISINORBEM
IURAQ:AMICITIÆHINCFIRMAUITDEPOSUITQ
ASSCITAANTIQUINISUSQ:TEXITIEMMORSCU
INLECEBRILUSUCIRCAIGNEMNOXIAENIMSIC
PELLAXDECIPITETSOCORDEMUBIIGNETOTA
CONSPEXITUOTOIÆARRIDENSUINXITAPERTE
OTUCRUXSPECIOSAOPUSPULCHRIOROMNIA
QUÆUINCTSNEMORAOCÆDRISALTIORIPSIS
MONSTRASNAMENUMERORADIANT.IDONABEATA
ADUENTUIESUSQUÆINTUSPROBUSOTIANUTU
ISTULERITDABATIISSEBEATECUMPIEUENIT
EGREDIENSUᵛUAHUCETBLANDONUMINESEMET
SIGNAUITCAELOSTERRENAETCONDEREREGNA
UTDUDUMSANCTILINGUACECINEREPROᶠETAE
FECERITHICCELSADOCTORDUMCONDIDITIMA
IMPERIŪINQ:HUMERISTANTOSITQUODPIEREGI

II.

SAINTS

THECLA
(Turkey, 1st century)

She was soon to be married, but as she sat by the window sewing, she heard a voice coming from the house next door: "Blessed are those who have kept the flesh chaste, for they will become a temple of God. . . Blessed are those who are self-controlled, for God will speak to them. . . Blessed are those who have wives as if they did not have them. . ." It was Paul, who had come to her city. She could not see him, but she sat for days listening, transfixed by his preaching.

Her mother and her fiancé could not get her to move from the window. Next door, a mob of men formed, angry that their wives and daughters were entranced by this message of chastity. Paul was arrested. She escaped from her house, bribed a guard to let her into the prison, and spent the night in his cell, listening to his words and kissing his chains.

They were discovered and taken before the governor. Her mother denounced her: "Burn the one who will not be a bride! Then all the wives who have been taught by this one will fear!" Paul was beaten and sent out of the city, but she was taken to the arena, stripped naked, and placed on a pyre. The flames rose, then were doused by a sudden cloudburst of rain and hail. The people scattered; she was unharmed.

She left the city, found Paul on the road, and asked to be baptized; he told her to be patient. They traveled together to Antioch. A nobleman, taken with her beauty, tried to buy her from Paul; when this was refused, he assaulted her. She resisted, tore his mantle and knocked off his crown. For this humiliation of an important man, she was led to another governor, and condemned to the arena to be eaten by wild animals.

A lioness ran up to her but lay at her feet. A bear tried to attack her, but was killed by the lioness. A lion charged, and both lion and lioness died in the struggle. There was a large pool of hungry seals, and she threw herself into it, declaring that, if no man would do it, she would baptize herself. Lightning struck and killed the seals. The women in the arena threw nard and cassia and cardamom into the ring and all the remaining animals fell asleep.

She was released and went looking for Paul. When she finally found him, he sent her off to preach. She was eighteen and went to live in a cave, performing miracles: storms were quelled, brigands met divine justice, temples of the Greek gods were destroyed, and many were cured of incurable afflictions.

The local doctors, nearly driven out of business by her miraculous cures, decided that the source of her power was her virginity. By now she was ninety and had lived in the cave for seventy-two years. They hired some drunken thugs to rape her. A passage opened in the rock. She walked in, the rock closed behind her, and she was never seen again.

Her shrine attracted crowds of pilgrims. In the fifth century, an author whose name is unknown was writing a book that recounted her life and the many miracles she had performed while alive and after her death. She came to him almost every night to supply him with the details. When his finger became infected and he couldn't write, she healed it. He tells how he had become neglectful, lazy, unable to continue. She appeared, picked up his notes and read them, smiling with approval, and told him to finish the book.

ANDRONICUS AND ATHANASIA
(Syria, 5th century)

He was a wealthy gold merchant in Antioch; she his wife. They were pious, dividing their wealth among the church and the poor. On Sundays, Mondays, Wednesdays, and Fridays, he would wash and care for poor men; she would wash and care for poor women.

Their two children became ill. He went to the shrine of St. Julian to pray for them, but when he returned home they were dead. She had a vision of St. Justin Martyr, who handed her a monk's habit.

They gave all their possessions to the church and set off for Alexandria. At the shrine of St. Menas, they parted. He joined the monastery of Abba Daniel at Scetis; she joined a woman's monastery at Tabennisi.

Twelve years later, he went to Jerusalem on a pilgrimage. There, he met a monk named Athanasius, who was actually Athanasia. Because of the perils of traveling as a woman, she had disguised herself as a man.

The years of austerity had altered them. She recognized him; he did not recognize her. She proposed that they travel together in absolute pious silence.

They returned to the monastery at Scetis and for the next twelve years silently shared a cell.

At her death, as they prepared her body, it was discovered that she was a woman. She left a note revealing who she was. He never knew. He died a few days later.

ANASTASIUS OF SUPPENTONIA
(Italy, d. 570)

For many years he was the revered abbot of the monastery of Suppentonia, built in the mountains under a giant rock and above a steep cliff. One day, he heard the voice of an angel calling him by name and summoning him. Then the angel called the names of eight other monks, each in turn. Anastasius died the next day, and the other monks, one by one, on the following eight days. A monk whose name was not called had begged him on his deathbed to be included, and he too died.

Another inhabitant of Suppentonia, who died some years before the others, was Nonnosus, also a saint. Some miracles are attributed to him: He instantly restored a glass lamp that had fallen and shattered on the floor. And when he wanted to grow cabbages on a certain piece of land taken up by a huge boulder, the boulder moved. Otherwise, it has been written that "he is not especially interesting in himself."

COLUMBA
(Ireland, d. 597)

He saw a young monk reading a book by a river, and he told the young monk that his book would fall in the water, and it did.

He foretold the arrival of unexpected visitors, the reign of kings, the sudden appearance of whales in the sea, the future lives of children he met, and the outcome of battles.

He could see behind himself. He could proofread the copies of sacred books without looking at them. When he chanted, his voice sounded normal to those next to him, but could be heard a mile away.

He knew that an evil man had slept with his own mother. Years before the news arrived, he knew that a town in Italy had been destroyed by a volcano. He knew that a priest was unclean, but didn't say how.

He did not ask Crónán the poet to sing, for he knew that same night the poet was to be murdered by brigands. He knew that Guaire, the strongest man in all of Dalriada, would be killed by a close companion, but he didn't tell Guaire that the companion was his knife that would slip in an accident. He knew that a wounded heron would land on their island and he instructed the monks to nurse it back to health when it was found. He stood in the sunshine and knew a storm was coming.

He knew that a youth named Colmán Ua Briún had not made the sign of the cross when he milked the cows and that the devil was hiding at the bottom of his milk pail.

He could cure plagues and heal broken bones and ease the pain of childbirth with a blessing. He could calm strong winds and high waves. With a prayer, he changed the heart of Luigne the Little Hammer's wife, who loathed and would not sleep with her husband.

Long after his death, in a great drought, his tunic was carried into the fields and shaken three times, bringing rain.

His biographer, Andomnán of Iona, wrote a century later that "by divine grace he had several times experienced a miraculous enlarging of the grasp of the mind, so that he seemed to look at the whole world caught in one ray of sunlight."

As a child, a ball of light was seen hovering over his head as he slept.

BRIEF LIVES (I)

Dathus
(Italy, 2nd century)
He became bishop of Ravenna after a dove miraculously appeared above him, but it is doubtful that he existed.

Genesius of Arles
(France, d. 303 or 308)
A decapitated martyr, his body was buried in France but his head was transported "in the hands of angels" to Spain, where he is invoked as a protection against dandruff.

Zoilus
(Spain, d. 304)
A young man martyred in Córdoba, he was vengeful after death: On his feast-day, an oblivious woman who was spinning found her right hand paralyzed, and a skeptical blacksmith mutilated himself with his glowing tongs; at the monastery named for him, animals that nibbled the monks' crops dropped dead.

Pelagia of Antioch
(Syria, d. c. 311)
She was a licentious dancing girl who converted, moved to Jerusalem, lived as a hermit on the Mount of Olives, and was known as the "beardless monk," whose sex was not discovered until her death.

Or she was a fifteen-year-old disciple of St. Lucian, who threw herself off the roof of her house to avoid imprisonment and rape when soldiers were sent to arrest her; St. John Chrysostom celebrated the "divine inspiration" of her courage, but St. Augustine said that suicide was not permitted, even under such circumstances.

Martin of Tours
(France, d. 397)
As bishop, he ordered the sacred groves to be chopped down, for "there is nothing religious in a tree trunk."

Syncletica of Alexandria
(Egypt, 4th century)
She cut off her hair and went to live in an unused tomb until she died at eighty-four, though it is said she suffered from spiritual desolation.

Paul the Simple
(Egypt, 4th century)
At sixty, he discovered his wife in bed with a neighbor, and left his farm to become a desert hermit; his nickname came from his childlike demeanor.

Onuphrius
(Egypt, 4th or 5th centuries)
He lived seventy years in the desert, dressed only in his long hair and beard, fed perhaps by angels.

Proterius
(Egypt, d. 457)
In the schism between the Coptic Orthodox and Greek Orthodox churches, he replaced Dioscorus as Patriarch of Alexandria, was lynched by an angry mob on Good Friday, his body dismembered and burnt, and was replaced by Timothy the Cat.

LAVSPIAPERPETVASANCTORVMINLVCESVPERNA
ADSISTERRIGENISALIQVIDQVODDICEREDIGNE
IAMDETEVALEANTAVIDAQVEIMPLEREDECENTER
ORABONISPOSSINTMODVLISETCANTIBVSALMIS
NEMPEEGOTECECINICRVXISTOINCARMINEVIVO
VERSIBVSEXOPTANSCANTANDOETREDDEREVOTA
SEOTVCVNCTASVPEREXCELLENSMVNERANOSTRA
MAIESTATEPOTENSVINCISTERRESTRIAVINCIS
SIDERACELSAPOLINECSATVALETVLLVSHONORI
NAMQVETVOFACERECONDIGNANECADOEREVERBA
TEMPTAVIQVELDEOHICEXCAELISMYSTICAVOTO
DVCEREVERBATIBICONTEMPLANSAPTAFIGVRAE
DISPOSVISIGNISOLSPERSOETTRAMITECADTVS
INSERVIANGELICOSINTEXIETVERSIBVSAPTIS
NEMPEAMENINMEDIOVITAESIGNACVLASPONDET
ALLELVICRVCISIRCVMDANSCORNVACONPLET
ETSACRAEEFFIGIEMCAELESTICARMINESIGNAT
NAMVTIHINCSCEPTRADVOTETMVNERATOTA
EXSVPERANTIARANTNVNCSPEIARDORVTORE
INMISSVSBONDETPALMAEETMORSILLAREMOTA
AVFVGIATPRIMAMNOCVITQVAELIVIDASTIRPEM
HVMANIGENERISTRVCVLENTAABSORBVITATQVE
PROGENIEMTOTAMETDETRAXITINIMAPROFVNDI
ATNOSQVOTQVOTAMORINCAELOSELEVATISTINC
RITESACRVMDOMINIPLACEMVSCARMINEVVLTVM
CARMINENAMQILLOQVOERITINSEDIBVSALTIS
QVODCANTANTIVSTICANTABVNTPERPETEVOTOET
HOCTVMRITEPLACETSIIMPLEMIVSSATONANTIS
MENTIBVSETSPECIEFACTISETFAMINELINGVAE
DAMTANTVMSERMOHAECIVSTINONPROEMIACARA
ACCIPIETSEDVERABENEPERFAMINAVIRTVSCVM
HAECLAVSDVNBONALAVSSEDVERFICTIOFALSA
SITQVAEMAGNACANITALTAVVLTPARVAMERETVR
ERGOAGEVOSCRISTVMLAVDATEFIDELITERODIS
CAELESTESPOPVLIVIRTVTESVOSQVEPOTENTES
IVSTORVMETPLEBESQIINCAELISISTITISARCE
PSALLITEAMENALLELVIAPERSAECVLACHRISTO

Brigid of Kildare
(Ireland, d. 523)
She used to hang her cloak on a ray of sun.

Sigismund of Burgundy
(France, d. 524)
A king, he murdered his own son but repented.

Ailbe of Emly
(Ireland, d. 528)
He could turn a cloud into a hundred horses.

Severus of Androcca
(Italy, d. c. 530)
Arriving too late to administer the Last Rites, he brought the man back to life again, so he could then die properly.

Vedast
(France, d. c. 540)
He resurrected a goose.

Teilo
(Wales, d. 560)
He was admired as the founder of churches and monasteries in Penally, Llandaff, and Llandeilo; at his death, all three places claimed him; they decided to ask Jesus which should house his remains, and the next day three identical corpses appeared, so that each could have one.

David
(Wales, c. 500– c. 589)
He had the gift of tongues, and when he went on a pilgrimage from Wales to Jerusalem he did not need an interpreter along the way.

Tigris
(France, 6th century)
From her pilgrimage to the Holy Land, she brought back the finger of John the Baptist.

DOGS AND CATS AND MICE

Christopher
(Marmarica, 3rd century)
In the familiar image on the medallions of travelers, Christopher carries the boy Jesus across a river. He was a gigantic man who lived as a Christian hermit by a river or he was a gigantic man who converted after carrying Jesus. In the story, he barely made it across: "You have put me in the greatest danger. I do not think the whole world could have been as heavy on my shoulders as you were." The child replied: "You had on your shoulders not only the whole world but Him who made it. I am Christ your king, whom you are serving by this work."

Historically he was from the North African tribe known to the Romans as the Marmaritae, was captured in the war against them and forced to serve with the Roman army in Antioch, where he converted. Refusing to pay tribute to Mithra, he was martyred. He lived centuries after Jesus and never by a river. His real name was supposedly Reprobus (Wicked), which may be allegorical; only centuries after his death it became Christopher (Christ-Bearer).

Marmarica was beyond the boundaries of civilization, and it was believed that its inhabitants were cannibals who had the heads of dogs. In the icons of the Eastern Church, he does not carry Jesus; he is portrayed simply as a martyr who happened to have the head of a dog.

Some think he was actually a Canaanite (*Cananeus*), who through a copying mistake became "dog-like" (*canineus*), but others consider this doubtful.

Sithney
(Brittany, 6th century?)
God asked him to be the patron of women seeking husbands, but he said he preferred to be the patron of mad dogs, which was simpler, and which he became. Mad dogs were given water from his well and were cured. People who suffered from the fear of water were also cured if they could be persuaded to drink the water from this same well.

Gregory the Great
(Italy, d. 604)
It was controversial whether hermits should have pets as companions. Jacobus de Voragine tells the story of a hermit "who had given up all for God and possessed nothing but a cat, which he petted and fondled in his lap almost as if it were a woman who lived with him." The hermit asked God where his austerities would lead, and God told him that he would come to live with Gregory, who was the pope, but one known for his humility.

"The hermit groaned with disappointment, thinking that his voluntary poverty was of little benefit to him if he was to receive his reward with one who enjoyed such an abundance of worldly goods. As he went on, day after day, grieving at the thought of his poverty and Gregory's wealth, there came another night when he heard the Lord say to him: 'It is not the possession of wealth but the love of it that makes a man rich. How dare you compare your poverty with Gregory's riches— you, who prove every day that you love that cat, your treasure, by the way you stroke it, while he does not love the wealth that surrounds him, but despises it and gives it away openhandedly to all who need it?'"

Gertrude of Nivelles
(Belgium, 626–659)
From an aristocratic family, she was the effective abbess of a monastery founded by her mother. She is the patron of those who suffer from suriphobia, the fear of mice, and is usually depicted standing placidly while mice run around her feet or up her crozier. No one knows why. In the 1980s, after her appearance in a catalog from the Metropolitan Museum of New York, she became the patron saint of cats and cat lovers.

JOHN CLIMACUS
(Egypt, 579–649)

A blind archer is useless.

A chaste man is oblivious to the differences between bodies.

A gloomy environment will cure pride.

A lemon tree lifts its branches upward when it has no fruit. The more its branches bend, the more fruit you will find there. The meaning of this will be clear to the man disposed to understand it.

A man in a fever ought not to commit suicide.

A man who has heard himself sentenced to death will not worry about the way theaters are run.

A royal crown is not made up of one stone.

A small hair disturbs the eye.

A well without water does not deserve its name.

An angry person is like a voluntary epileptic.

Crabs are easy to catch, for sometimes they walk forward and sometime backward.

Dried-up mud draws no pigs.

I don't think anyone should be classed as a saint until he has made his body holy, if indeed that is possible.

I knew a man who sinned openly but repented in secret. I denounced him for being lecherous but he was chaste in the eyes of God.

If you are in a crowd, seek out dishonor.

It is dangerous to climb a rotten ladder.

It is hard to drive a dog from a butcher's shop.

It is risky to swim in one's clothes.

Remembrance of wrongs is far removed from natural love, but like a flea hidden on a dove, it may live next door to fornication.

Snow cannot burst into flames.

Take a hard stone with sharp corners. Knock it and rub it against other stones until its sharpness and hardness are crushed by the knocking and rubbing and, at last, it is made round.

The cypress tree does not bend to the ground in order to walk.

The man who is seriously concerned about death reduces the amount of what he has to say.

The sleepy are easily robbed.

The sun is bright when clouds have left the air.

Those who take mud in exchange for gold are suffering a loss.

Waves never leave the sea.

When we draw water from a well it can happen that we inadvertently bring up a frog.

EUPHROSYNUS THE COOK
(Egypt, 9th century)

A poor Palestinian, he left his village as a boy and wandered begging. A monastery outside of Alexandria took him in and put him to work in the kitchen. He was illiterate, seemingly unintelligent; the monks treated him badly. He often stood at the back of the church as they chanted, not understanding a word, gazing at the icons.

An elderly priest came to live at the monastery after his retirement. One night he dreamed he was in Paradise. A figured appeared: it was Euphrosynus the cook. The priest asked the cook if he could take something from that beautiful garden and the cook picked three apples and wrapped them in a kerchief.

When he woke, the priest wondered at his dream and thought it only a dream. Then he saw the three apples by his bed. He went to Euphrosynus and asked him where he had been last night. The cook replied: "The same place as you."

The priest gathered the monks to tell them the story. They went to the kitchen to honor Euphrosynus, but he was gone.

JUAN GARÍN
(Spain, 9th century)

He lived as a hermit in a cave in the mountains, performing austerities. Satan, jealous of his piety, assumed the form of another hermit, living in a nearby cave.

The Count of Barcelona, convinced that his beautiful teenaged daughter was possessed, sent her to Juan to be exorcised. Urged on by his fellow hermit, Juan asked the girl to stay with him in his cave. Lust overwhelmed him. He raped her, then cut off her head and hid her body.

Realizing what Satan had made him do, he cried out to God and traveled to Rome to beg forgiveness from the pope. The pope told him that in penance he must live as a beast until the day when a four-month-old baby would pardon him.

He crawled like an animal back to Spain, living on leaves and scratching for roots. Hair grew all over his body; the fur was matted with dirt. Seven years passed.

Then he was discovered by a hunting party, who marveled at this strange beast. They put a rope around his neck and took him to the city. Crowds came to look at him. Among them was the new wife of the same Count of Barcelona, carrying her four-month-old baby in her arms.

The baby suddenly spoke: "Stand up, Juan! You are forgiven." He stood up; the hair disappeared from his body.

He confessed his crime and led them to the cave. They exhumed the count's daughter and found her alive, unaged, and with only a hairline scar on her neck from her beheading. She vowed never to marry, became a nun, and later was the abbess of the monastery the count built on the site.

SOLETLVHADEVMHICCHRISTVMENBENEDICITEIESVM
CRVXESTVESTERHONORSTABILISLVXPACIFERORDO
LVXSTROBITASSERIESPERCVNCTAETSAECVLALVMEN
VOSQVEDIEMHACNOCTEMAVESIMVLPERPENDITISORA
STRINGITISATAHVIVSCENTELADVIHCVLAGRESSVM
STIRPSQVEHABETHAECENOSDECIESETRINQIESVNVM
ABOTHOROINPROPRIOECIESQVOQVERITETRICENOS
YAMQVENISSOLROTAVESENOSCITVRINBERELVHAET
TEMPORAQVENISTOTAETSEMELOMNISCIRCVITANNVS
SINOSQVEETDECIENSQINOSHABETHISCLOBOSORBES
SEPTIMANAEATQVEHABETVNIVSAVORELIMITISORAM
AMHOSADHANCQDIEMVERSVMTENEROMNESETORDOHIC
IAMHVCREERVADRANSALISCRVXTOTAQEMNOTATARTE
QVATYERETSAENISARCECIRCVMVOLATVMBRISQVAE
ADRESCVNTNVMEROINVITVSQEMOSTENDERITETSOL
CALVESVPERVICVMHOCECCEAEQVINOCTIASIGNANT
YTSACRATIIPSOCLARADIEORNASCVNCTATENEBRIS
CRVXOQVESANCTAMICASHINCENETCHRISTVSVBIO
ORICRVCISCOMPLEYCESISIBASBARATHRVMORVGVARI
ARTOORDINESCEPTRVMHACATRVELAETHERACELSAMANT
HAECQVEDECVMVNDIESSEMREGITASTRAPOLIHINC
DONATMAGNASALVSHOCSEDEHAECLAVSTRAQVECAELI
LAVSHOMINVMHABESODISPLANATCVNCTADIGIHAVSTA
ATQVESACRAMETELCIEMHOSTISINARDVASISTITIESVM
NAMIVDAEAFREMENSSAVISEXCVLITARBOREPOMMET
QVOHOCPOSSENTETRAGONIQVAEREREPARYIBORBIS
GENTESETPOPVLIEXAYTVORMARISVNDIAVESVMMIS
HAECQVEDAPESVITAEMONSTRANTVRDECRVCECVNCTIS
QVODSALIENTVRIBIETYDECIESDECVPLATARESVMANT
DONAPATRISSVMIATQVENOVENOSTVMAETHERECERNANT
ARGELICOSPOPVLOSOSINGVLITVNDIAVEFVLGEANT
HINCMONEOVTCANTOTOSPIASSCRIPTARVEAGAMVS
QVATINOSEXITIVMSDECVMMORSASPERAINORBEMHVO
IAMFREMITHACPELLIHADEEXILIOHINCVLEAYIAM
POSTVOQVEREGNADEIETSVPERALAMLVCENITENTES
PRENDAMVSLAETIHINCRERVMETRESONEMVSOVANTES
AVCTOREMCHRISTVMDOMINVMOMNIPOTENTISETALMI
NEMPEPATRISNATVMQVERVDALMVMATQARCESVPERNVM
SITQVOQVEHAECNOSTRARAYIOLAVSSEMPERETARDOR

BRIEF LIVES (II)

Mo Lua of Killaloe
(Ireland, d. c. 609)
Although an ascetic himself, at the king's banquet the beer was making the guests vomit, so he dipped his shoe in the barrel to purify it and the festivities went on.

John the Almsgiver
(Cyprus, c. 552–620)
He never spoke an idle word.

Rumwold of Brackley
(England, d. c. 650)
Only three days old, at his baptism he suddenly spoke and delivered a sermon on the Holy Trinity and the need for virtuous living, then died.

Fiacre
(Ireland, c. 600–670)
Although, or because, he was a celibate who barred women from his meticulously kept gardens, he is the patron saint of those suffering from venereal diseases.

Cuthbert
(Scotland, c. 634–687)
After standing all night in a freezing river as penance, two otters warmed and dried his feet.

Landelin of Ettenheimmünster

(Germany, 7th century)

A forest hermit, he was killed by a hunter who mistook him for a deer.

Gangulphus of Varennes

(France, d. 760)

When he discovered that his wife was having an affair with a priest, he became a hermit in his own castle, practicing austerities until the priest murdered him.

Gummar

(Belgium, d. c. 775)

It was said that it was God's plan that he would marry a woman so malicious, extravagant, and oppressive, that he would be forced to leave her and become a hermit devoted to God.

Theodore and Theophanes Graptus

(Jerusalem, 775–841 and 778–845)

Anti-iconoclast brothers who were monks, the emperor Theophilus ordered that a twelve-line insulting poem be tattooed on their faces.

Donald

(Scotland, 8th century)

He lived a devout life with his daughters, the Nine Virgins, after his wife's death, but his obscurity makes his popularity as a name for boys puzzling.

Richardis

(France, c. 840– c. 895)

Her husband, the mad Emperor Charles the Fat, accused her of adultery; she consented to an ordeal of fire, walked barefoot wearing a shirt of wax through the flames and was unharmed; she left and joined a nunnery.

Elijah Speleota

(Italy, 863–960)

A girl possessed by demons was taken to his tomb in the cave where he had lived; she fell asleep; he appeared and took a "crooked little thing" from her mouth and killed it; she was cured.

Dunstan of Canterbury

(England, 909–988)

To distract him from his prayers, the devil appeared to him as a bear, then as a wild dog, then as a "foul fox with a twitching tail," then as a man who wanted to talk about women.

Oswald of Worcester

(England, d. 992)

Bishop of Worcester, archbishop of York, he died on his knees in his daily practice of washing the feet of twelve poor men.

WEDDINGS

Wilgefortis
(Portugal, date unknown)
There was a famous painting in Lucca of Jesus on the cross wearing a long tunic rather than a loincloth. It was explained that this was not Jesus at all, but rather the daughter of the king of Portugal, whose name was Wilgefortis or Liberata or Livrade or Kümmernis or Ontkommer or Uncumber.

She was one of sextuplet sisters and had taken a vow of chastity. Her father insisted she marry the king of Sicily. She prayed to be saved and a beard suddenly grew on her face. The Sicilian sailed away, rather than marry another sister, and her father had her crucified.

Oda of Rivreulle
(Belgium, d. 1158)
She wanted to be a nun; her aristocratic family insisted she marry. A suitable match was found; the dowry paid; the wedding dress sewn; the decorations hung; the banquet prepared. The groom recited his vows; she remained silent. A kindly relative, assuming she was merely modest and shy, urged her to speak. She said she could marry no other, for she was already vowed to one "from whose embraces I can never be separated, not by love of another, or gifts, or the threats and blows of my parents." The groom and his family stormed off. She went into the house, found a sword, and cut off her nose, so no one would ever think of marrying her.

Nicholas Politi
(Sicily, 1117–1167)
As a newborn, he refused to nurse on Wednesdays, Fridays, and Saturdays.

Still a boy, he could heal sheep with a prayer and drive away wolves by
making the sign of the cross over them.

He was to be married at seventeen, but on his wedding day an angel
helped him to escape.

As he fled, an eagle fed him along the way.

Satan appeared in the form of a wealthy merchant, and tried to convince
him to return to the wedding celebrations; he resisted.

The eagle led him to the entrance of a cave on Mt. Etna, where he spent
the next thirty-three years in extreme austerity.

The angel would tell him when someone was coming to look for him, so
he could hide.

AELRED OF RIEVAULX
(England, 1110–1167)

What are you doing, what are you doing?
Why are you distracted by this and that?
Why do you seek so many things?
How can there be delight in this place of terror and desolation?
How can you find knowledge in this land of the shadow of death?

Do you love this world?
    You are greater than the world.
Are you blinded by the sun?
    You are more blinding than the sun.
Do you wonder about the motion of the stars?
    You are above the stars.
Do you hope to unravel the mystery of the beginning of life?
    No life began more mysteriously than yours.
Is your mind confused when you try to think about these things?
    You yourself are the most confusing of all.

MECHTHILD OF MAGDEBURG
(Germany, 1207– c. 1282/1294)

The Lord said: "Look, you are like this tiny animal."

This animal was brought forth on an island in the sea out of the slime. The sun was the animal's father, the sea its mother, and the slime its matter.

This animal does not eat. It has a large tail that is full of honey that it sucks on every day.

This animal at times has a desire to drink from the sea and it cannot regain its health unless it urinates and gives back the bitter seawater.

This animal has big ears and it listens for the songs of birds.

This animal cannot remain in the sea when animals do their mating dance. It hurries up the highest mountain it knows and climbs to the top of the most beautiful tree it sees and clasps the lofty trunk.

This animal has two sharp horns to defend itself.

This animal has two beautiful human eyes that pour forth tears.

This animal has a soft mouth and a pure tongue, but it does not have teeth. It cannot snarl nor bite.

This animal is swift of foot and has no voice.

This animal's skin and hair are of a common color and faded and ugly. No one hunts it. But after its death, when the other animals rot, its skin and hair become so beautiful that all the most prominent people that can obtain it wear its coat rather than the finest sable.

This animal's flesh is eaten on Fridays. It does not die unless it is beaten to death by the waves of the sea.

This animal's bones are the skeleton of a fish. From it one can fashion beautiful jewels that noble persons wear in honor.

This animal's name is Alles Nutze, Everything Serves.

PETER OF KORISHA
(Kosovo, 1211–1275)

Although the parents were pious, they were disturbed that their son would not play with other children; he spent his days in prayer. He resolved to devote himself to God, but his father died and he could not leave his mother and sister without support. Although an ordinary laborer, he wore a hair shirt under his clothes. When his mother died, he tried to marry off his sister; she insisted that she would follow him and share his life of purity. They moved to a local church and lived in adjoining cells, fasting and praying. There were too many friends and relatives in the village interrupting their contemplation; they left for the mountains.

He felt that his sister was an obstacle in his effort to serve God, but she insisted on following him. The journey was long and one night, as she was deep in sleep, collapsed from exhaustion, he made the sign of the cross over her forehead, prayed that God would protect her, and left weeping. When she awoke, she prayed, "Holy Mountain of God, have mercy upon me. I am alone. I do not want to return and live in the world. Neither am I worthy to live and see my brother. I beg that I find death in you." Later, when the news of her heavenly repose reached him, he thanked God for receiving her.

He lived in a cave on the side of a cliff, ate wild plants in the summer and snow in the winter, and saw no one. He showed no mercy to his body, practicing great austerities, for he wanted to cleanse himself of his passions and give himself as a pure offering to God.

He was tormented by a demon who would come into his cave in the form of a snake. It spoke to him in the voice of his sister, begging him to save her from wild animals. Despite his prayers and fasting and hymns sung loudly to drown out the voice, the snake would not leave him alone. He prayed for help from an angel and suddenly an angel full of light appeared, took him by the hand, and said: "Do not be afraid. I am Michael, archangel of the Lord's army. Because of your prayer, God has sent me to punish the cunning snake that is harming you." Michael drew his sword and chased the snake away. He wept: "I am black with passions, and give off a vile stench because of my sins. Who am I, Lord, that Thou should send me Thine most glorious and splendid Archangel?"

He practiced even greater austerities, wounding himself with sharp rocks, and yet the demons continued to torment him with unclean visions and thoughts of pride and vainglory. The demons came to his cave in the guise of a flock of ravens. He knew they were intending to gouge his eyes out, but he drove them away with prayers.

He grew old, filled with the joy of divine light. The demons no longer approached him. He knew they were afraid of the grace that God had granted to him.

Some monks came, for God did not want a man such as this to die unnoticed by the world. He asked them to dig his grave, and then he lay down in it.

```
T E P A T E R A L M E P O L I D O C T O R E M C A R M I N E I N I S T O
R E C T O R E M Q U E U O C O F E L I C I B U S A N N U E C O E P T I S
T U P I U S E T C L E M E N S S E N S U M D A N S U E R B A Q · C A S T A
U T T U A Q U I D P R I M A S I G N E T L E X P A N D E R E P O S S I M
A D C R U C I S A E T E R N A M L A U D E M L E G I S Q S E C U N D A E
I U S D E M O N S T R A N D U M U O T A R I T U S Q U E P E R E N N E S
C U M P R I M U M H A E C R I [T E G E N E] R A T I O M A X I M A R E R U
E X O R T A E S T E X I N U I [S I S C R U] C I S A L M A R E F U L S I T
G L O R I A C U M D O N O L U [X A L M A B] E A U I T E T A R M A H A E C
C U N C T A S I M U L R E C R E [A T T U A] Q N U N C D E X T E R A X P S
E T U E R A L U C I S D A N S [M U N E R A] C U M C R U C E S A E C L I S
N A M G E N E S I S U I T A E [L A U D A T] M I R A B I L E L I G N H O C
I N T E R C U N C T A F U I T P L A N T A T U M Q U O D P A R A D I S O
U I U I F I C A N S L I G N A T R I B U E N S E T M U N E R A F R U C T
H O C P A T R I A T Q · I S A C U E X I T M U L T A N D U S A D A L T A R
O R A T E [E X O D U S] H O C [I U R A S A] T I S [A S T N U M] E R O R U M
E U E H E R A [T Q U E C] U I [C E R D O T] I U M [E R U S C A] N I T O R E
N U P T A C [A N I T T R] I U I [I S L E U I] B : [N T A T M A] R E L U D :
U D A T T R A [N S I T U] H O S [T I C U S O B] M A [G N A L I A] C A N T A T
E T P L E B [S C A R M E] N I O [P T I M E P] U R E [M I R A T R] O P H A E A
L A U D E [N A M O R E] D Ï P [S A L L I T] Q · T R I U M P H I E T E O U M
H O C M A R E T E S T A T U R U I C T R I C E S O R B I T A C A L L E S
A T U E T E R E H O C L I G N U M L E G I S D U L C A U I T A B Y S U M
B I S P E T R A M E X C U D I T U I U A M P R O D U X I T E T U N D A M
N A M Q U E A M A L E C H C A [N A M D E U] I C I T P R I M I T U S I R A
S I G N U M H U I U S P A R I [T E R N O M] E N D E L E U I T E T I L L I
B O T R U M H O C U E C T E P [I U M R E N] O T A U E X I T U T E R Q U E
U E C T O R U M U O T I S E T [O U A N T I] B U S O M N I A L A U D A N T
D O N A D E I T E R R I S H I [S G A U D I] A I N E S S E P U L A R U M
Q U I S B E N E M Y S T E R I [A D I C I T] U E L D I C E R E C U N C T A
R I T E U A L E T C R U X D O N A T U A C U I N O N S A T I S O M N I S
L I N G U A C R E A T U R A E P O T E R I T D E P R O M E R E L A U D E
H O S T I A T E P A T R I S A E T E R N I D E D I C A U E R A T A R A M
U I T A E S E R P E N T E M E X A L T A S T I E T T U P I E C R I S T U
M O N S T R A S T I P O P U L O D E T E L T Q I D D I C E R E P O S S U
C U N C T A B O N A D E D E R A S D E M E B A S E T M A L A C U N C T A
```

HADEWIJCH*
(Belgium, 13th century)

I saw a queen, wearing a gold dress, and her dress was full of eyes, and all the eyes were transparent, like fiery flames and yet like crystals. The crown she wore on her head had as many crowns, one above the other, as there were eyes in her dress.

She approached me dreadfully fast and put her foot on my neck, and cried out in a terrible voice: "Do you know who I am?"

And I said: "Yes! Long have you caused me pain and woe. You are my soul's faculty of reason."

*Hadewijch has not been canonized by the Church.

AGNES BLANNBEKIN
(Austria, 1243–1315)

Although called a saint by many, the Vatican never recognized her. She was a poor peasant who became a nun and practiced extreme fasting in solidarity with the suffering of the world and of Jesus on the cross. She was considered strange and was disliked in the convent. As she was illiterate, her visions were dictated to an anonymous Franciscan confessor.

She saw monks and nuns and Jesus himself naked. The Lamb of God kissed her. She pressed her lips against the spear-wound on Jesus' side and drank the blood. She could taste Jesus' body in the Eucharist. She told her confessor that she "was filled with an excitement in her chest every time that God visited her that was so intense that it went through her body and that it burned as a result, not in a painful but in a most pleasurable manner."

Of her most famous vision, her confessor wrote:

> Crying and with compassion, she began to think about the foreskin of Christ. . . And behold, soon she felt with the greatest sweetness on her tongue a little piece of skin alike the skin in an egg, which she swallowed. After she had swallowed it, she again felt the little skin on her tongue with sweetness as before, and again she swallowed it. And this happened to her about a hundred times. And when she felt it so frequently, she was tempted to touch it with her finger. And when she wanted to do so, that little skin went down her throat on its own. . . And so great was the sweetness of tasting that little skin that she felt in all her limbs and parts of the limbs a sweet transformation.

BRIEF LIVES (III)

John Gualbert
(Italy, c. 985–1073)
A dissolute noble, he set out to avenge the murder of his brother, found the killer on a Good Friday and forgave him; an image of Christ on the cross bowed its head to acknowledge his charity and he became a monk.

Eskil
(Sweden, d. c. 1038)
East of the village of Tuna, he disrupted a blood sacrifice, urging them to repent, and they stoned him to death.

Dominic Loricatus
(Italy, 995–1060)
His parents had given the local bishop a deerskin to obtain his ordination as a priest, and he spent his life doing penance for it, lashing himself hundreds of thousands of times as he recited the Psalms.

Arialdus
(Italy, d. 1066)
Because he preached against simony, the archbishop sent him to an island in Lake Maggiore, where he was killed by two priests.

Anno of Cologne
(Germany, 1010–1075)
A powerful archbishop, his death was so painful that some said that God would not have made him suffer such punishment if he had led a good life.

Stanislaus Szczepanowski

(Poland, 1030–1079)

He excommunicated King Boleslaus the Cruel, who then killed him in church with a sword as he was celebrating Mass.

Nicholas the Pilgrim

(Greece, 1075–1094)

He wandered the streets carrying a cross and shouting "Kyrie eleison!"; was followed by packs of children imitating him; was considered mad; but after his death at nineteen, miracles began to happen at his tomb.

Gerlach

(Holland, d. c.1170)

He lived inside a hollow oak tree and became famous for his sanctity, incurring the jealousy of the monks at a nearby monastery; they spread a rumor that he was keeping a treasure buried under the tree; the bishop ordered it cut down, but no treasure was found.

Drogo of Sebourg

(Flanders, 1105–1186)

A wandering shepherd, he became so deformed that his appearance was frightening the villagers; a windowless cell was built for him adjacent to a church, where he lived for forty years without being seen.

Rainerius

(Italy, 1117–1160)

Formerly a strolling minstrel, his austerities became excessive and God had to remind him to eat.

Gerard of Clairvaux
(France, 1120–1177)
A strict disciplinarian as abbot, he was murdered by a monk he had ordered disciplined.

Peter Spanò
(Sardinia, 12th century)
He prayed in a thorn bush.

Walhere
(Belgium, d. 1199)
A parish priest, he was killed by his nephew, a parish priest.

William of Rochester
(Scotland, d. 1201)
He was a baker or he was a fisherman who was on his way from Scotland to the Holy Land, but only got as far as Rochester, Kent, where he was robbed and murdered.

Idda of Toggenburg
(Switzerland, d. c. 1226)
A raven stole her wedding ring; a hunter found it in a nest; her husband saw the hunter wearing the ring, accused her of adultery and threw her out the castle window; angels saved her and she became a nun.

Elizabeth of Thuringia
(Hungary, 1207–1231)
At her death, mobs cut off pieces of her clothes, hair, nails, and her nipples to keep as relics.

Ilona

(Hungary, d. 1240)

When she received the stigmata, a circle of gold appeared on her right hand and out of it grew a white lily.

Hermann Joseph

(Germany, c. 1150–1241)

Of modest intelligence but extraordinary good looks, he imagined he was a knight and the Virgin Mary his lady; in a vision she gave him a wedding ring and the other monks began to call him "Joseph."

Isnard

(Italy, d. 1244)

Heretics mocked him, asking how an ascetic monk could be so fat.

Placid of Rodi

(Italy, d. 1248)

He slept standing for thirty-seven years, for to lie down was to submit to carnality.

Honoratus of Buzançais

(France, d. 1250)

A wealthy cattle merchant, his servants robbed him, then killed him as he explained to them the nature of sin.

Adolf of Osnabrück

(Germany, 1185–1284)

A charitable bishop, Hitler was named after him.

Franco Lippi
(Italy, 1211–1291)
Escaping prosecution for murder, he joined a gang of thieves; at fifty, he was blinded in a fight, walked barefoot to Santiago de Compostela where his sight was miraculously restored, then walked to Rome dressed in a sackcloth and lashing himself with a whip.

ANGELA OF FOLIGNO
(Italy, 1248?–1309)

While looking at the cross, I was given an even greater perception of the way the Son of God had died for our sins, and this was extremely painful. I felt that I myself had crucified Christ. This perception set me so on fire that, standing next to the cross, I stripped myself of all my clothing and offered my whole self to him. I promised him then to maintain perpetual chastity and not to offend him again with any of my bodily parts, accusing each of these one by one.

I then prayed to God to enable me to shed all my blood for love of him as he had done for me. I was even disposed to wish that all the parts of my body suffer a death that would not be like his, but one much more vile. I imagined and desired that if I could find someone to kill me, then I would beg him to grant me this grace, namely, that since Christ had been crucified on the wood of the cross, that I be crucified in a gully, or in some vile place, and by a vile instrument. Moreover, as I was unworthy to die as the saints had died, that he make me die a slower and even more vile death than theirs. I could not imagine a death vile enough to match my desire.

This fire of the love of God became so intense that when I heard anyone speak of God I would start screaming. People thought I was possessed, but even if someone had stood over me with an ax, this would not have stopped my screaming.

I was still living with my husband, and it was bitter for me to put up with all the slanders and injustices. I bore them as patiently as I could. Then it came to pass that my mother, who had been a great obstacle to me, died. In like manner my husband died, as did all my sons, in a short space of time. Because I had already entered the way of the cross and had prayed to God for their deaths, I felt a great consolation when it happened. God had granted me this favor, and my heart would always be within God's heart, and God's heart always within mine.

MARGARET OF CITTÀ DI CASTELLO
(Italy, 1287–1320)

She was born blind, a hunchback, a dwarf who could barely walk. Her aristocratic parents had hoped for a son; ashamed, they kept her hidden in a locked room. At sixteen, she was secretly taken to a church in another town where miracles had occurred. There was no miracle, and her parents left her on the steps. A poor family found her and took her in. She was kind and wise and helped the local children. She joined a convent, but the nuns were cruel to her and she returned to the poor. Another convent invited her and she remained. At her death at thirty-three, they dissected her heart and found three pearls.

```
NATEPATRISSUMMIQUITELAFEROCIAFRANCIS
DAMIHIRITECRUCISUICTRICIACARMINAFARI
NTACAELESTANIMALMI    SUOLATOREIOHANNIS
TRANSPENETRANSAQUILAETUEROOMINEUIDIT
EOUMSOLUERBUMHABSITINARCEPOLORUMHOC
CRATIASICQ:IOHANNIAHTEOMNESQUIDAFATU
DONATAUTQ:ARTHOMINISIBISUMERETAUCTOR
SCRIPSERITATQE        PIODSUNUSETALM
SEMCUPATREQUI         ITAQUESALUSQUE
SITNATUSFACTUSQUECARODOMINATORINORBE
HUNCLEOHUNCUITULUSREGEDANTPONTIFICEQ
UTLEOQUIFORTISRETULITCERTAMINEPRAEDA
HOSTIAETOBTULERATSUMUSSERITESACERDOS
MYSTYCADONASUISCONSORTIB:OPTIMEDONANS
NEMPEDATORUMMISTERIOSEPTEMETPIEPANUM
DATMARIS          QUOQEUIUIDECANTU
OTURREGEAIUT  TECGEAGHU  DAPIELUOS
HOCSIGNAT&FR  SDEIECCEA  PONTIFICEQUE
DAT&HEDSQUITOLLITQ        ES    DIS
FOR      MANUSETPARECEDI
INBETHLEECENITMATREADMIRABILISINFANS
IPSESATUSMARIAMINDOUTISSIMACURAHUIC
NOBILISATQUEPUERPERSONAUETUSTADIERUM
QUIUENITDEEDOMDEBOSRAHICUESTECRUENTA
CALCATURUSERATQUISOLUSTORCULARAUCTOR
INCRUCEPENSAND:QUISUSTINETASTRASUPERN
UTCRUXALMAFORETDIUINOHAECMUNEREDIUES
NASCRIBENSBENEMATTEUSDEDITORDINEPRIM:
QUIINFACIEFIRMATUISHUNCABORICINEDAUID
PROCENITESSEHOMINEMSICNAUITQMPIEUOTU
QUODCEN:HOCDEDERITPISTILLOFRAUDISINIQ
EXPULSONAMRITE       USOMNERETEXTUM
CONTINETHOCUER       SCREDERESIGNUM
NEMPEDICETDUDUCRISTUSQUIANASCIERILLA
PROMISSUSSTRIPESTSALUATORMAXIMUSORBI
```

RITA OF CASCIA
(Italy, 1381–1457)

The day after her baptism, bees were seen swarming around her crib, climbing in and out of her open mouth; she was unharmed. A child bride, she had her first baby at age twelve. Her husband was violent, uncontrolled, and engaged in a blood feud with another family that had lasted for generations. They murdered him. At the funeral she asked that they be forgiven and she thought the vendetta had ended.

Her husband's brother took her two sons to live with him. They grew up to be like their father and uncle, violent and uncontrolled, and they vowed revenge on their father's death. She asked God to prevent them from committing this mortal sin; soon after, both sons died of dysentery. She thanked God for keeping them from an eternal life in Hell.

She asked God to save her husband's brother. He came down with the plague, survived, and renounced his violent ways. The vendetta finally ended.

At thirty-six, she was transported by levitation into the garden courtyard of the monastery of Saint Magdalene, where she lived for the next forty years. Jesus took a thorn from his crown and pierced her forehead; the wound was visible for years.

CATHERINE OF PALLANZA
(Italy, 1437–1438)

Her entire family had died from the plague. At fourteen, Jesus appeared to her and told her he had found a home for her in the mountains above Varese. She moved into a cave and rarely ate. Every day she read the same passage in the Gospel of John on the Passion of Christ. Every Saturday she said a thousand Hail Marys. Little else is known about her life in the cave.

She wanted to be alone, but years later she was joined by Giuliana Puricelli, an illiterate peasant from a nearby village, who had run away from her violent father. All that is said about her is that she was patient and would fetch water for visiting pilgrims. She also would become a saint.

Three other women came, and then more, and a community of hermits was formed.

DOGS AND CATS AND A TROUT

Bernard of Clairvaux
(France, 1090–1153)
His mother dreamed she was pregnant with a barking puppy. She consulted a priest, who told her: "Don't be afraid; all is well. You will be the mother of a fine puppy, a guardian of God's house, who will bark loudly on its behalf against the enemies of the faith."

(He did not, however, have the dog called St. Bernard named for him; that was another saint, Bernard of Menthon, who opened a hostel for pilgrims on their way to Rome in a high mountain pass in the Alps.)

An omen of future sainthood, the mother of Vincent Ferrer (Spain, 1350–1419) also heard barking from her womb.

Guinefort
(France, 13th century)
He is a saint who was actually a dog. A knight and his wife, unknowingly reenacting a story from the *Panchatantra* (which reached Western Europe in the 11th century, having traveled from Sanskrit through Persian, Syriac, Arabic, Hebrew, and Greek to Latin and Spanish) went out and left their infant son in the care of their faithful grayhound, Guinefort. When they returned, they found blood splattered, the crib overturned, and the dog's mouth bloody. Enraged that the dog had murdered their child, the knight drew his sword and killed it. Then he heard the baby cry. It was under the crib, and next to him, the body of a viper that the dog had attacked to save him.

The knight built a shrine to Guinefort. He placed the dog in a well, covered it with stones, and planted trees around it. Women came with their infants to be protected by the saint. Some time later, the inquisitor Stephen of Bourbon visited. He was told that the babies were passed back and forth between the trees, then laid down on a bed of straw with candles burning on either side of their heads. The mothers had to leave their children until the candles burned down. Sometimes the unprotected babies died from the cold, sometimes the straw caught on fire and killed them.

Stephen had the shrine destroyed, but the cult of Guinefort lasted there, outside of Lyon, until the Second World War.

Francis of Paola

(Italy, 1416–1507)

He was named after Francis of Assisi and followed in his footsteps, creating a movement that became known as the Order of Minims. The word referred to their style of life, to their humility, and to their profession that they were the "least of the faithful." They built several large monasteries.

He had a pet trout named Antonella. A local priest threw breadcrumbs in the pond to lure it, then took it home to cook. Francis sent a monk to find the trout. The priest angrily threw his frying pan on the ground and the cooked fish broke into pieces. The monk gathered them up and took them back to Francis, who placed them in the pond and prayed, "Antonella, in the name of Charity, return to life." The fish swam again. Francis chastised the priest for his hungry greed in stealing and cooking the fish and chastised Antonella for its hungry greed in coming to eat the breadcrumbs.

Philip Neri

(Italy, 1515–1595)

Known as the Third Apostle of Rome (after Peter and Paul), he was famed for his joyfulness and sense of humor. He ate no animals or the products of animals. His heart was so big that at his death it was discovered that some of his ribs were broken. He loved music, created the idea of the Oratory—a place for sacred musical dramas—and was a patron of Palestrina. He was attached to his cat, which he lived with in his cell and carried around the city in a basket.

When the pope made him relocate to another monastery, he declared that care for his cat would be a form of penance for the young monks he left behind. He would frequently summon them to question them about the cat, which was interpreted as a means to break down their vanity and pride.

BRIEF LIVES (IV)

Vanna of Orvieto
(Italy, d. 1306)
Her heart burned so intensely that she took off all her clothes to pray and still was drenched in sweat; when she went into a rapture, stretched out as though on the cross, mosquitoes would land on her unblinking eyes.

Frederick of Regensburg
(Germany, d. 1329)
Although not a monk, he chopped wood at the monastery.

Imelda Lambertini
(Italy, 1322–1333)
At eleven, as she received her First Communion, a glowing host was seen by all above her head; she stayed on after Mass to pray. Hours later they found her still kneeling, smiling, and dead. It was said that she had often said: "Tell me, can anyone receive Jesus into his heart and not die?"

Flora of Beaulieu
(France, 1309–1347)
The other nuns ridiculed her, for she was usually silent and depressed but sometimes ran screaming down the corridors; then one day they saw her hovering in the air with her arms outstretched and blood streaming from her mouth and sides.

Villana de'Botti
(Italy, 1332–1361)
She led a life of extravagance until the night, dressing for a party, she saw in the mirror the face of a demon rather than her own, and became a nun.

Romeo
(Italy, d.1380)
A monk who died of the plague on a pilgrimage to the Holy Land, his name was oddly or randomly appropriated by Shakespeare.

Roland de'Medici
(Italy, 1330–1386)
A Medici, he renounced his family, went to live unsheltered in the forest, dressed in a goatskin, and never again spoke a word.

Panacea de'Muzzi
(Italy, 1368–1383)
At fifteen, she was killed with a spindle by her wicked stepmother who discovered her praying instead of doing her chores.

John Nepomucene
(Bohemia, d. 1393)
King Wenceslaus IV had him drowned when he refused to say what Queen Sophie had told him in confession.

Margaret the Barefooted
(Italy, d. 1395)
In solidarity with the poor, she dressed in rags and never wore shoes, winter or summer, and her husband despised her for it.

Peter Gambacorta
(Italy, 1355–1435)
He converted twelve robbers who became the Poor Brothers of St. Jerome; when his father and two brothers were murdered, he refused to leave his cell and forgave the assassin.

Mary Mancini of Pisa
(Italy, d. 1431)
At five, she was transported to the cell where Peter Gambacorta was being tortured and cut the ropes binding him; at twenty-five she had lost two husbands and all her seven children; the actual Catherine of Siena came to visit and as they prayed together they were surrounded by a bright cloud out of which a white dove flew; she became a nun.

Thomas Bellaci
(Italy, 1370–1447)
At seventy he went to preach in Syria where, to his regret, he was not martyred, and he returned to Italy to die.

Peter Capucci
(Italy, 1390–1445)
A friend of Fra Angelico, it is said that the most remarkable thing about him was that he always preached with a skull in his hands.

John of Sahagún
(Spain, 1419–1479)
He preached against extravagant clothes, and women would pelt him with stones on the street; he preached so severely against sex outside of marriage that a woman poisoned him when she lost her repentant lover.

John Soreth
(France, c.1420–1471)
He reformed the Carmelites to admit nuns; he was mistaken for Ethiopian; he died from eating unripe mulberries.

```
SANCTABEATAPOTENSUITAELAUSGLORIACHRISTI
CRUXUENERANDADEITUPROSPERAFUNCTIOSAECLI
DIGNABONAATQUEPIAXPOAFICERASQUIAMEMBRA
STIPITESUSPENSAFFLICTOSSUBCARCERISUMBRA
DERIPERASPOPULOSREGNUMINSUBLIMEREPOSTUM
QUISDEDERASQUONIAMSPECTATIOLONGAPOLORUM
REDDITAIUREPIISBEATOLIMETSTEMMATEDIGNUS
NAMBONAQUAEINTERRAMPIUSARBITERORESERENO
SEMINADISPERSITSACRAMULTIPLICAUITAMAUIT
QUAEQUESEDENSMONTISORAUITINARCEMAGISTER
DISCIPULISTRIBUENSPACTUMPIAFOEDERATURIS
INCIPIEBATENIMALMIFICOTUNCORDINESANCTIS
UIRTUTUHISTITULISDOMINUSPIAPANDEREDICTA
UTBENEDICTAPATRISPROLISHOCDOGMATESIGNET
CRUXQUIATOTABONACONPLECTITETOPTIMAPERSE
DATDOCETALMAANNECTITAMANTIBUSATQUEBEATA
SICFELIXDIUINAMARDORETREMENSPREMECORDAM
QHICESFACETIUSTITIAMHOSTEPIOALCIDASERUA
FLENTESQUICUPIDOSNAMHISSURSUMENADEUMQ
QUISCONSULAETERNAACSITMISERATIOCERNENT
DOLATIOIDQREFECTIOPASTIOLARGAAETINARCE
NONALTOACTIOCONPETITOREREPENSQESUPERNU
OPSESTNUNCUALETHICATQHOCSATISINTERNACUM
LONGEABSUNTHUMILLUESOLQUODPRONUSADORAT
CUMUERBUMHAUDSOLUMMITESSEDINORDINEMORES
OMNITENENSPOSCITSEMPERHOCTEMPOREQUEOMNI
ERGOBEATORUMESTHABITAREINLUCEUOLENTUMET
OCTENOHOCNUMEROUTSUPERARDUADONAREQIRANT
HOCQRESURGENTESREGNUMQUIASICCRUCEUADENT
CRUXUIASCALAROTAPATRIADUXPORTATRIUMPHUS
UITABEATAHOMINUMMERITORUMETMAXIMAMERCES
BINAQUATERPOSITAENREGNIPIAFORMULAPANDIT
SANCTABONOSBENEDONAPOLUMSCANDENDOMERERA
CUNCTIPOTENSQEDEIDOMINUSHOCOMNIPOTENTIS
SPIRITUSIPSEMODISUULTPACISSCANDERESEDEM
SEPTENOSQGRADUSSUPERISEREXERATASTRISQUO
ALTAPOLIHINCPITEPOSSEBENIGNOSPANDERETIRE
QUOSCOMITATURAMORRATIOLUXLAUSBONAUIRTUS
GLORIASTEMMATHRONUSQUISADDITURARCEPOLO
```

Anthony Neyrot
(Italy, 1425–1460)
A Dominican priest, he was captured by Moorish pirates on a sea voyage, taken to Tunis where he converted to Islam, began to translate the Qur'an, married a Turkish noblewoman, repented, put on his old Dominican robes, climbed the steps of the palace and, as he proclaimed his faith before the king and court, was stoned to death.

Eustochium Bellini
(Italy, 1444–1469)
Born to a nun from a "degenerate" monastery and raised by nuns who thought she was a witch and imprisoned and starved her, at her death it was found she had branded the name of Jesus on her breasts.

MAGDALENA OF THE CROSS
(Spain, 1487–1560)

A devout child, at the age of five she was praying in her church in Córdoba when she heard beautiful, ethereal music and a handsome young man with long black hair appeared before her. He was assumed to be Jesus himself, and word spread through the city.

She had visions; she fell into ecstasy. She made a lame man walk and a deaf man hear. Someone looked in her eyes when she was in a trance and saw the heavens and the Holy Trinity and the Communion of Saints. Terrified by her notoriety, she ran away from home to live in a cave and her guardian angel carried her back to her bed. Jesus appeared again to tell her that she was destined for great things, but that she should modify her severe penance and take care of her health. Ignoring him, at age ten she tried to crucify herself on a wall. Dying from the infected wounds, on Easter Sunday she tore off her bandages and said that Jesus had cured her.

She stopped eating, but seemed healthy. She whipped herself bloody, but the wounds healed overnight. Strangely, two of her fingers had not grown; they remained the size of a small child's. Some believed those were the fingers Jesus had touched in her first vision.

At seventeen she joined a Franciscan convent. She carried a heavy cross around the convent, kissed her companions' feet, ate only the daily communion wafer. Her fame spread. On the day she took her vows and became Magdalena of the Cross, the archbishop himself came to the ceremony, and rather than exhorting her to Christian piety, as is usual, he asked her for her prayers. A dove descended from the ceiling of the cathedral, landed on her shoulder, and seemed to speak into her ear. Then it flew outside and rose straight up into the sky. The news traveled, people all over Spain wrote for help from her prayers, donations poured into the convent. She predicted various events that all came true.

Then, on the day of the Feast of the Annunciation in 1518, she told her abbess that she was pregnant. She had never left the convent; the only man she saw was her confessor. Rumors circulated; her stomach grew; she increased her mortifications, whipping herself and walking on broken glass. The archbishop sent three midwives to examine her; her virginity was intact. Ignatius Loyola and a few others were skeptical, but it was decided that God works in mysterious ways and that this might well be the first Virgin Birth since Mary.

On Christmas Eve she announced that she was about to give birth, but that her guardian angel had told her she must do this completely alone to increase her suffering. She was locked in a little house; the whole convent prayed.

She later told them that at midnight she had given birth to a magnificent child who radiated blinding light; the cold air of her chamber had become warm. Her hair suddenly grew very fast so she could swaddle the child in it, and it miraculously turned from black to blonde and then to black again. (She still had a few of the blonde curls she had cut off, which she gave to the nuns as relics.) But on Christmas morning, she found herself alone, the baby gone, her breasts chapped from suckling. The midwives were called in again, and confirmed that she indeed had the marks of childbirth.

Thanks to this miracle, her convent became the richest in Spain. Charles V, Holy Roman Emperor and King of Spain, and Queen Isabella asked for a piece of her habit to wrap around their own expected baby, the future Prince Philip II, in order to give the royal child the "assistance of a living saint from birth, to envelop him in Divine grace." The archbishop consulted Magdalena on the construction of a new cathedral and largely used the convent's overflowing treasury to build it.

She was made the abbess of the convent and imposed severe mortifications and penances. The nuns were to crawl on their knees and make the sign of the cross with their tongues on each other's shoes; cord whips were replaced with iron-tipped ones. Contrary to the tradition that self-mortification should be done in darkness and solitude, Mother Magdalena ordered that the nuns perform it with candles lit and in front of the others. They were encouraged to wear crowns of thorns and belts with spikes pointing inward, to kneel on nail-studded boards, to stretch out on the floor and have the other nuns walk over them. They were ordered to confess to graver sins than they had ever admitted, but as for Magdalena herself, St. Francis had appeared before her and told her she no longer needed to confess at all.

She was far more famous than her contemporary, Teresa of Ávila. The queen sent Magdalena her portrait; the king asked her to bless his banner before he set off on a military expedition; cardinals came to visit her; the pope asked for her prayers. But she became increasingly unpopular inside the convent, instituting rules—personally mandated to her by the Virgin Mary—that no one liked, refusing admission to girls from prominent families on the grounds that they had Jewish ancestors, indulging her favorites and punishing the others.

In 1543, she fell seriously ill and was near death, normally the moment for a confession of one's entire life. But as soon as her confessor put on his stole, she went into convulsions. It was suspected that she might be possessed by demons. An exorcist was called. He noticed that in her ecstasies her eyes were not fixed, one of the hallmarks of true rapture. He stabbed her with a needle and she had no reaction. Then he dipped the needle in holy water and stabbed her again. She moaned, a sure sign of possession.

She was told she would not live to see the next Christmas. She suddenly sat up in bed and cried out: "1544! The forty years as announced! I am a cursed dog! Take me to Hell!" She screamed "revolting blasphemies," rose into the air and was suspended there.

Another exorcist was called. Horrible words and demonic laughter issued from her mouth. The cardinal ordered an inquisitor to investigate, and gradually the story was revealed:

The beautiful young man she had seen as a child was not Jesus, but a devil named Balban, who turned into a shimmering mist and then into a monster with a toothless mouth, a wide, flat nose, and twisted horns, and then back into a beautiful young man again. He promised her fame for forty years if she consented always to obey him; he left the mark of the devil on the two fingers that never grew.

The Inquisitor made the sign of the cross over her and she rolled on the floor, "striking indecent poses and mimicking the vile copulations that she had performed with Balban for nearly forty years." The cries of ecstasy that the nuns had so often heard coming from her cell were the sounds of this satanic lovemaking.

It was Balban who secretly fed her all the years when she claimed to eat nothing but a communion wafer. Her pregnancy was a cruel joke they had played on the nuns and the clergy. She was impregnated with a monstrous caterpillar, which "escaped from her body with a loud wind that famous Christmas night, before changing into Balban, and re-possessing her with unprecedented vigor."

Exorcised and repentant, Magdalena was sent to prison. She begged the Inquisition to consign her to the flames, but it was decided—perhaps to save face among the many influential people she had deceived—that the fault was the demon's, influencing a young child, and that this pact with the devil had finally ended after forty years.

She was sent to another convent, where she lived for many more years in blameless expiation for her sins. In the end, "the great and small of her time were all later sure that her final deep humility and repentance had made her quite worthy of Paradise."

HYACINTHS*

Hyacinth of Caeserea
(Cappadocia, d. c. 120)
In prison, the only food he was given was meat that had been consecrated to idols, which he refused to eat, and he starved to death. The jailers saw him comforted by angels. He was twelve.

Hyacinth of Porto Romano
(Italy, 2nd century?)
A martyr, his existence is only probable.

Hyacinth
(Egypt, d. c 257)
He lived with the hermits of the desert, then went to Rome, where he was beheaded.

Hyacinth of Paphlagonia
(Anatolia, 3rd century ?)
He cut down a tree sacred to the pagans and was tortured to death.

Hyacinth of Fara
(Italy, date unknown)
A martyr about whom nothing is known.

Hyacinth Odrowaz
(Poland, 1185–1287)
Appointed by St. Dominic himself, he spread the Word, and founded churches and monasteries in ceaseless travels through the "outposts of

ÆLESTESPLÆBESET LARASACCIPISILLI
ÆGNAREGENDOPOLIC UCIfIXINUT;ETARDO
NDIQTEALMIfICATR BEASCŪSANGVINISUS
RISTIQUAPROPTERE REGEUOCABERETUDU
UMQEHUMANATIBIEX UIRISDIUINAQTACT
NIUSALTITHRONIDE OTOINLAUDISHONOR
RISTICOLASSOCIAS TSACROfAMINEUIUA
ULTIPLICESLAUDES NDASACULMINECAEL
NTERRISCANTUSQUO OffERTORBISETEXU
ANCTIfICATMUNDUS MENT;TEPONT;ETHICSO
XALTATIUBILANSCŪ ONTIBUSARIDACANT
URACANUNTSTELLIS OTUTUCARMINADONA
RTUSETOCCASUSAQU LOSICAUSTERETAUR
ÆTITIAMREGNITENC ASQUODLUMINELUME
LTAPOLIPANDASCON IGNESNUMENETISTI
ANTADEIDONADISPE SANSQUIOMNIAfECI

UANTATIBIDEDERAT ANTORŪfACTORAMOR
IQIfICANTISENIMD NODEUSIPSEPARAUI
TBENETEXTULERAT IRENEDICEREPUPPU
ANCIDUSISUALEATD CEPTORDUXETINIQU
XEMPTAMRISITPRÆ AMQILUCISABAÆTHR
ETRUSAMQEDIUUOLU TPUNIRENECANDOHI
NPIACRUXDOMINIDE ANTANSQUISPIEMUS
AÇNIfICAREUALETT NTÆTEETDICEREfAT
ULCHRANITÆSCULTU ÆUISUÇLORIACINÇI
AXUSDIRAfUGITCAL MUSSETPINUSHONOR
NCLINANTHUMILESE CEDROSMŸRRAMELŸRO
LfACTŪPAUITANTNA DUSETMIRACŸPRESU
ÆXTIXTUSÇUTTAAMM MUMBALSAMABIDELL
ICTÆMAIESTATESU ERSAUOTAfERUNTTÆ
OMINETUASPERIORM IORUIRTUTEPIISHO
ONASCUMMERCEDEME NTXPIANTETRIBUNA

civilization": Eastern Europe, Prussia, Russia, Turkey, Greece, Scandinavia
—where he slept in the snow—and, it is said, though there is no record
of it, Tibet and China. Wherever he preached, he spoke in Polish but the
people miraculously understood him.

When the son of Princess Przybislauska drowned in the river, he
brought him back to life. He provided miraculous pierogi during a famine.
He restored the sight of two children who were born without eyes.

In the Mongol sack of Kiev, as he was rescuing the ciborium holding
the Blessed Sacrament from the monastery, the Virgin Mary asked him to
take her too. He carried a stone statue of her, larger than himself, and led
the faithful to the banks of the Dnieper. He told them to follow him to
safety and they all crossed dryshod. His footprints remained on the surface
of the water, and for centuries could be seen whenever the river was calm.

Hyacinth Orfanel
(Spain, 1578–1622)
A Dominican sent to Japan, where he was burned alive.

Hyacintha Mariscotti
(Italy, 1585–1640)
Her lover, the Marquis Cassizucchi, married her younger sister, and she
became so petulant that her parents sent her to a convent. She escaped,
was returned, and for ten years was considered impossible by the nuns,
ignoring the rules, asserting her aristocratic privilege, receiving visitors in a
lavishly furnished cell with a private stock of food. She became ill, was told
by her confessor that she was serving the devil, and suddenly reformed and
led an austere life. Then she reverted to her scandalous ways. She became
ill again and, according to her hagiography, turned into "a model of heroic
patience, penance, prayer, untiring goodness, sweetness, and promptness
in serving all. From that time she gave herself to a life in which cruel
disciplines, constant fasts, deprivation of sleep, and long hours of prayer
all played their part." She is liturgically celebrated as a virgin.

Hyacinth of the Angels
(Mexico, c. 1660–1700)

He and his friend John-Baptist were Zapotec laymen charged with suppressing Zapotec rituals. Hearing that a ceremony was taking place, they intervened and confiscated the ritual objects. The next day they were attacked by an angry mob, who cut open their chests with machetes and, as the Aztecs had once done, extracted their hearts.

Hyacinth Castañeda
(Spain, d. 1773)

A Dominican monk, he was sent to Asia: a long sea voyage to Mexico, where he was ill the whole time; a long march across Mexico; a longer sea voyage to Manila, where he was ill the whole time. Manila had been captured by the English, and it took him months to find the other missionaries. Then to China, where missionaries had been recently martyred. The Chinese deported him to Vietnam, where he was tried and beheaded. At his trial, a spectator supposedly called out, "We'd believe him if his Lord of Heaven came down and set him free."

Hyacinth Cormier
(France, 1832–1916)

As a youth, he was musically talented, played the flageolet, the organ, and the ophicleide, and was praised by Franz Liszt, who heard him perform. He wanted to join the Dominicans, but suffered from chronic hemorrhage, and there were fears of tuberculosis spreading in the monastery. Yet his piety was such that his superiors appealed to Pope Pius IX, who said that if he could last for a month without an incident he could be ordained. On the 29th day he had an attack that was so severe, it was decided to ordain him on his deathbed. The pope declared "since it is not for him to live under the religious habit, it will be at least for him to die under it." He recovered, lived on for fifty years, founded orders and colleges, oversaw convents, wrote the biographies of eminent Dominicans, and levitated while in prayer.

*(Hyacinth the flower sprang from the drops of blood on the ground from the slain Hyacinthus, and was a Christian symbol of rebirth through the blood of Christ, as well as prudence, peace of mind, and the desire for heaven. It was ignored that Hyacinthus was a beautiful Spartan prince, the lover of Apollo, who died in a game of quoits, either accidentally or through the jealousy of Zephyrus, who also lusted for him. At his death, according to Ovid, Apollo wished he were mortal and could join him.)

BRIEF LIVES (V)

John Marinoni
(Italy, 1490–1562)
He delivered thousands of sermons, all on one subject: the Crucifixion.

Robert Bickerdyke
(England, d. 1586)
An apprentice laborer, he was seen in a pub buying a priest a glass of ale, and was executed in York.

Catherine dei Ricci
(Italy, 1522–1590)
Thousands came to her monastery every Thursday through Friday to watch her go into a trance and reenact the Passion, with her shoulder deeply indented from carrying the cross, and wounds appearing where she was scourged and stabbed, where she was crucified, and where the crown of thorns had been placed on her head.

Francis Caracciolo
(Italy, 1563–1608)
He was wasting away from leprosy when he decided to become a priest and was instantly cured; at his death it was discovered that his heart was completely shriveled and that it had the words *Zelus domus Tuae comedit me* (The zeal of Thy house hath eaten me up) inscribed on it.

Francis Zirano
(Italy, 1564–1603)
A monk, he traveled to Algeria disguised as a merchant to ransom his cousin who had been captured by pirates; he was discovered and flayed alive, his skin stuffed with straw; his cousin, however, escaped.

Germaine Cousin
(France, 1579–1601)
Born with a deformed hand, suffering from scrofula, beaten by her cruel stepmother, forced to live in the barn with the sheep, friendless, illiterate, she prayed.

Peter Claver
(Catalonia, 1581–1654)
In Cartagena in the Kingdom of New Granada (Colombia), a center of the slave trade, he spiritually freed 300,000 slaves by baptism, instructing them with a triptych painting: in the center, Jesus on the cross; on the right, "a group of Negroes, glorious and splendidly arrayed"; on the left, "the wicked Negroes, hideous and deformed, surrounded by unlovely monsters."

Isaac Jogues
(France, 1607–1646)
A missionary in New France, captured and tortured by the Mohawks and made their slave, deep in the winter he had a vision that he was in a bookshop covered in crosses and bought a book that contained, a voice told him, "the acts and deeds of men illustrious in piety and of hearts brave in war," and he knew that one could only "enter into the Kingdom of Heaven through many tribulations."

Mary-Anne-of-Jesus Paredes y Flores
(Ecuador, 1618–1645)
She lived as a recluse in her own home, helped in her mortifications by an indigenous servant; after the earthquake of Quito, she offered herself as a victim for the city and died a few days later; a white lily sprouted and bloomed from her blood.

Dominic Higashi
(Japan, 1626–1628)
He was beheaded in Nagasaki at age two.

Anthony Grassi
(Italy, d. 1671)
It was noted that his manner became more serene after he was struck by lightning, which also cured his severe indigestion.

Mary of the Angels Fontanella
(Sardinia, 1661–1717)
A Discalced Carmelite nun, she bound her tongue with an iron ring and suspended herself on ropes in the shape of a cross.

PHILOMENA
(place unknown, date unknown)

In 1802, the tomb of a young woman was discovered in the catacombs of Rome, marked by three tiles that read:

LVMENA PAXTE CVMFI

Below the tiles were paintings of two anchors, three arrows, a palm and an ivy leaf. It was assumed that the tiles were out of order, and should have read:

PAXTE CVMFI LVMENA

("Peace with you, Philomena"). And it was assumed that Philomena was a virgin martyr from the early centuries, although her name was not included in the Roman Martyrology (the Church's comprehensive list of saints) nor in any contemporary or medieval accounts.

The remains were translated to Mugnano del Cardinale, in southern Italy, where a new church was built with a sanctuary containing the relics. Miracles occurred: A statue sweated blood for days. Pauline-Marie Jaricot, the French founder of the Society of the Propagation of the Faith and the Living Rosary Association, was cured of a terminal illness on a pilgrimage to the church. The dust of her bones multiplied, providing relics for hundreds of reliquaries.

In 1833, she appeared to a nun in Naples and told her story: She was the daughter of a Greek king who had converted to Christianity. When she was thirteen, the emperor Diocletian (who reigned from 284–305, the most notorious of the persecutors of Christians) fell in love with her. She had taken a vow of consecrated virginity and refused to marry him. She was tortured. She was tied to an anchor and thrown in the river, but two angels cut the rope and carried her to the shore. She was shot three times with arrows: the first time, her wounds instantly healed; the second time, the arrows turned aside; and the third time, they turned around and killed the archers. Finally, she was decapitated on a Friday at three in

131

the afternoon, the same time that Jesus died. This explained the tomb's decorations of two anchors, three arrows, a palm leaf (traditional symbol of the victory of martyrs or of the victory of the spirit over the flesh), and an ivy leaf (symbol of fidelity).

Through the 19th century her reputation spread, although she was never officially canonized. Pope Gregory XVI declared a feast-day; Pope Pius IX a mass and office dedicated to her. The Confraternity of Saint Philomena was founded in Paris, then raised to an Archconfraternity by Pope Leo XIII, then raised to an Universal Archconfraternity by Pope Pius X. In his Apostolic Brief, *Pias Fidelium Societates*, he ordained that "The current statements [regarding the historical authenticity of St. Philomena] are and remain always fixed, valid and effective; in this way it has to be judged as normative; and if it is proceeded in another way, it will be null and void, whatever its authority."

Authority, in the form of archeologists and ecclesiastical historians, however, raised doubts in the 20th century. The tiles belonged to the 2nd century; the bones to later in the 4th, when Christians were no longer persecuted. It was common, in those same catacombs, for old tiles to be used to seal tombs, and thus their misarrangement. And, of course, before 1802, no one had ever heard of Philomena. The Sacred Congregation of Rites ruled in 1960 that her name should be removed from all liturgical calendars. The National Shrine of Saint Philomena, Miami, Florida still objects: "The action taken in 1960 [was] the work of the devil in order to deprive the people of God of a most powerful Intercessor, particularly in the areas of purity and faith at a time when these virtues were so much being challenged as they continue to be up until now!"

JOHN VIANNEY
(France, 1786–1859)

He escaped the draft into Napoleon's army by hiding in the mountains under an assumed name in a community of deserters. When an amnesty was declared, he resumed his studies for the priesthood. He was ordained, but could never master Latin and was not considered bright, so he was sent to a village with only two hundred inhabitants. He stayed for over forty years.

The villagers had lost their faith during the Revolution and the Terror. He restored the church, started an orphanage, and persuaded them to give up the sin of dancing. St. Philomena, to whom he was devoted, cured him of a serious illness; he built a chapel and a shrine in her honor, and urged the parishioners to pray to her.

Word of his sanctity traveled. Twenty thousand pilgrims a year came to his village, and he would spend eighteen hours a day in the confessional, where his consul was usually a single revelatory sentence. Six hundred lay people and three hundred priests attended his funeral. He became the patron saint of priests.

In 2018, his incorrupt heart was taken on a six-month "Heart of a Priest Nationwide Relic Tour" of the US. The organizer of the tour explained: "The church in the United States is wounded now, and we are praying for our priests, and looking to a saint who was a model of virtue and dedication to his ministry to help us through this period of injury and to renewal." A priest in New Haven, Connecticut, was more explicit: "Essentially the Church in recent months in this country is going through difficult times. The sexual abuse crisis, the clergy sexual abuse, is very much in the headlines and on the hearts of many of the Catholic faithful. I felt it important that we as a parish gather together in this way for several days of prayer—to pray for the crisis, to pray for our Church, and to pray for God's blessings for what we're going through right now."

BRIEF LIVES (VI)

Mary-Margaret d'Youville
(French Canada, 1701–1771)
The widow of a swindler who traded alcohol for furs with the Iroquois, she founded the Grey Nuns, who built hospitals and orphanages with the large number of slaves the congregation owned.

Benedict Joseph Labre
(France, 1748–1783)
Rejected by various monasteries as unsuitable, he wandered homeless to the major pilgrimage sites of Christendom, dressed in rags and rarely speaking; in his last years he slept in the ruins of the Roman Colosseum.

Dominic Savio
(Italy, 1842–1857)
A schoolboy who died of tuberculosis, he had a vision of a multitude of people groping their way across a dimly lit plain; then the pope appeared holding a torch, and a voice proclaimed: "This torch is the Catholic faith which shall bring light to the English people."

Stephen-Theodore Cuénot
(France, 1802–1861)
A missionary in Vietnam, he died of neglect in the imperial stables, chained to the elephants.

Mary-of-Jesus Deluil-Martiny
(France, 1841–1884)
She founded the Association of the Guard of Honor of the Sacred Heart, now known as the Association of the Presence of Christ, and the Daughters of the Heart of Jesus, and was shot to death by the convent gardener, considered an anarchist, on Ash Wednesday.

Francis and Jacinta Marto
(Portugal, 1908–1919 and 1910–1920)
They were aged nine and seven, guarding the family sheep when the Virgin Mary appeared to them in the hills outside of Fátima; nevertheless, he died at eleven and she at ten.

Francis Dachtera
(Poland, 1910–1944)
A priest, he died from the medical experiments performed on him at Dachau.

YOUNG TERESAS

1.

Teresa Kim-I
(Korea, d. 1837)
A pious virgin, she was strangled in prison with six other Christians. Age unknown.

Teresa Kim
(Korea, d. 1840)
A pious virgin, she was strangled in prison after her parents had been killed. Age unknown.

Teresa Manganiello
(Italy, 1849–1876)
A pious virgin from a peasant family, she was known locally as the "Wise Illiterate of Montefusco." She hoped to found a new congregation devoted to helping the poor, but died of an unknown illness. She was twenty-seven.

Teresa Chen Jinjie
(China, 1875–1900)
A pious virgin, she was stabbed to death by Boxers while on her knees in prayer. She was twenty-five.

Teresa-of-Jesus Fernández Solar of Los Andes
(Chile, 1900–1920)
A pious virgin, she entered a convent but died of typhus before she could become a nun. She was twenty.

Teresa Demjanovich
(USA, 1901–1927)
A pious virgin from a family of Ruthenian immigrants in New Jersey, she hoped to become a nun, but died shortly after of appendicitis in a hospital in Newark. She was twenty-six.

Teresa Bracco
(Italy, 1924–1944)
A pious virgin from a peasant family whose village was raided by German troops. A soldier dragged her into the fields; she resisted; he strangled and shot her. She was twenty.

2.

Thérèse of the Infant Jesus and of the Holy Face
(France, 1873–1897)
Her family was pious; her four older sisters were nuns; she was the last remaining daughter. Her father had a mental breakdown, threatened her with a gun, and was institutionalized. She was then given permission at the age of fifteen, which was unusual, to join her sisters in the Carmelite convent in Lisieux.

She was shy and unremarkable, a model nun in her compliance to the rules and duties. Her life was uneventful. She had no visions; she performed no miracles nor practiced spectacular austerities. She wrote a few religious poems, two plays about Joan of Arc for the nuns to stage among themselves, and some spiritual meditations. She believed that God was not a cruel judge, but a loving Father, perhaps unlike her own. Her favorite metaphor was the newly-invented elevator, and she believed that one could rise up to God not only through great works but through small everyday acts of kindness and love. In her last years she suffered from the ravages of tuberculosis and died at twenty-four. On her deathbed, her sister Céline told her: "You are my ideal, and this ideal I shall never be able to reach."

Céline and her sister Pauline—now Mother Agnes, the abbess of the convent—vowed to make that ideal known to the world, and they both lived long lives, dying in the 1950s, to accomplish the task. Within a year after her death, Mother Agnes cobbled together the scattered writings, made 7,000 revisions and additions to the text, and published it as Thérèse's autobiography, *The Story of a Soul*. Céline took charge of the iconography, as the impact of visual images had again become evident in the Church with the first photographs of the Shroud of Turin in 1898 and the success of St. Bernadette of Lourdes, the first extensively photographed saint.

Mother Agnes had allowed Céline the rare privilege of having a camera and a darkroom in the convent, and she had often photographed their sister. In her first effort at posthumous representation—the frontispiece for the autobiography—she heavily retouched one of her portraits to give the rather plain Thérèse an ethereal glamour.

An ally, Monsignor Roger de Teil, told her that she needed more than a "simple bust": an attribute was necessary to represent "the devotion of believers with a mark of its own." Céline came up with the icon of "Thérèse of the Roses," roses being a perennial Catholic symbol, with their color like the blood of Jesus, their thorns likes his crown, and their heavenly fragrance and beauty. She collaged and retouched a photo of Thérèse, slightly smiling with a beatific gaze, holding a crucifix covered with roses. Another placed Thérèse meditating in a rose garden. Her last words were now reported as "At my death I will let fall a shower of roses." She became known as the Little Flower.

Céline modeled her work on the popular, old-fashioned sentimental religious imagery being produced on the rue Saint-Sulpice. She altered her photographs to copy the Saint-Sulpicean versions of various saints, changing Thérèse's clothes or inserting her into familiar deathbed tableaux. Artists were commissioned, and they produced scenes of Thérèse cuddling the baby Jesus, Thérèse at Joseph's carpentry shop with the child Jesus running toward her, Thérèse with Joan of Arc, even—to the displeasure of some in the Church—Thérèse as an angel with the Holy Family and, more scandalously, Thérèse's face as the Virgin in an Annunciation scene. She was shown performing miracles

```
SANGUINISERGOSACRINOSTFUSIOLAUITETUNDA
SORDIB;ACUNCTISDETERSITETOMNIACHRISTUS
NOXIANAPASSUSLABESTULITHICQUOQ:NOSTRAS
DELENSARATUMCONTRAORBEMTUMCIROGRAPHUM
LUMENEUANGELIIIMITABILECONDIDITAUCTOR
QUODFACIN;SCRIPTOUETATOMNIAUANARECUSAT
QODUITAMSIGNANSINCUNCTOEXPENDITURORBE
LUMENUIRTUTUMASCENSUETDOMINANTISUBIQE
INDICATORATUMPANDENSQUOMISTICASCRIPTA
MONSTRANTDONADEIQUANTAOMNIB;OBTULITORE
ASTDECIESDUODENATENETHICLAUDACARACTER
GRAMMATANECHOCUNASEMELSEDHOCQUATERUNA
MAGNANOTANSFIDEIMISTERIAMAGNAQUEFIDIS
GAUDIADEMONSTRANSMEDICINAEMUNERAGRATA
ETSOCIALEDECUSQUODSPIRITUSAUCTORINORE
ARDENSLUXDEDERATCONCORDIMUNERELINGUAE
HINCQUEALACERCOETUSSACRATUMIACTATUBIQ:
HOCNOMENRETEEXPANDENSQUODSACNAINABYSSO
MUNDIPLENAALTARETRAHATFRENETUTOMNES
HISFRENISCRUCISUTQINSIGNIACRISTUSUBIQ:
DIGNECOMMENDETHOMINIQUAEMAGNARESIGNAT
INMULTISDONAADIUNGENSPROBAPROEMIANATI
ENORBISDOMINIQUICONDITPRAEMIAINAUCTE
MULTIPLICATDIGNISIUSTECUMPATRESUPERNO
REGNATORREGNANSCUNCTADICIONEGUBERNANS
QUIPIGNUSDEDERATPARACLITUMIURESALUTIS
UTREGATETSERUETPERDUCATADTRIAUITAET
PSALLITEDEUOTEUITAMBENEPSALLITECRISTO
GENTESACLINGUAEUERUMETCOGNOSCITEREGEM
UIRTUTEMQ:PATRISQUAOCCUMBITDIRAPOTENTI
MORSQ:SUIETSTIMULIRERUMSCITOTEPARENTEM
HAECLAUSCULMENHABETEXUEROGERMINEPARTA
AETERNAMREQIEMISTEESTNATURAEINDITORDO
SERUETUTINDITATANTUMETSPERETDONABEATA
GLORIAHAECUIRTUSETSUMMAESTCAUSAQIETIS
ISTEQUIURABENECONSERUATLIBERACHICEST
QUIBONASUMMACUPITRITEETMEDIOCRIADUCIT
```

among missionaries in the Congo or rescuing a car going off a cliff. Céline maintained strict control over all the images and even sued the makers of other ephemera.

The success of the book and the images led to an industry, monopolized by a single company dedicated solely to creating Thérèse devotional items. There were shelves of spinoff books and pamphlets for adults and children, devotional cards to carry in a purse or wallet, postcards, lithographs, calendars, souvenir albums, exercise books, writing paper and blotters, short silent films, lockets, charms, badges, brooches, scarf pins, necklaces, bracelets, medallions, napkin rings, and gift boxes to hold them.

Simultaneously, Mother Agnes employed her connections to the most powerful elements of French Catholic conservatism, from the anti-Dreyfusards to Charles Maurras and the Action Française, all of whom used Thérèse as a rallying-point against the secular government and the anticlerical factions of the fractious first decades of the century. With the onset of World War I, she was refashioned as a beacon for the French troops, portrayed bringing the light of God and scattering roses on a battlefield or ministering to a dying soldier. There were postcards of soldiers making a pilgrimage to Thérèse's grave emblazoned with her supposed words "I love France, the Fatherland." (In World War II, Agnes' connections to the Vichy government led to the sisters producing images of Thérèse showering rose petals on Marshal Pétain.)

Pope Pius X, who died in 1914, had already prematurely called her "the greatest saint of modern times." His successor, Pope Benedict XV, dispensed with the required fifty-year delay between death and beatification. She was declared "Venerable" in 1921, beatified in 1923, and canonized in 1925 by Pope Pius XI, only twenty-eight years after her death and, remarkably, only five years after Joan of Arc was finally declared a saint. The celebration for Thérèse was far more elaborate than that held for the heroine of France. Long-neglected customs of decoration were revived; hundreds of workmen spent weeks hanging the dome of St Peter's with torches and tallow lamps; 60,000 people crowded into the Basilica, and half a million gathered in St. Peter's Square.

Although she never left her convent, in 1927 she was named Co-Patron of the Missions, with St. Francis Xavier. In 1944 she was named Co-Patroness of France, along with Joan of Arc. In 1997, she became the youngest Doctor of the Church—an honor that, at the time, had been given to only thirty-two saints since 1298 for significant contributions to theology and doctrine. (Among the men were Augustine, Thomas Aquinas, and John of the Cross, and there were only two previous women: Teresa of Ávila and Catherine of Siena.) Both of her parents were also declared saints—the only married couple to be simultaneously canonized in the history of the church—and one of her other sisters remains in the process toward sainthood.

Her basilica at Lisieux became second only to Lourdes as the most-visited shrine in France. (At seven, Edith Piaf was cured of blindness there.) In her centennial year of 1997 it received two million pilgrims. A waxworks museum with dioramas of her life opened in Lisieux in 1929, and in the town one can buy Thérèsette, a table liqueur, St. Thérèse paté, and St. Thérèse boudin. Among many others, biographies of her have been written by such disparate writers as Vita Sackville-West, Dorothy Day, and Kathryn Harrison.

Her relics continually travel the world, including a visit to South Africa in 2010 to coincide with the World Cup. The astronaut Ron Garan took a relic on the Discovery space shuttle, circling the globe for two weeks, for she had supposedly said: "I would like to travel over the whole earth to preach your name and to plant your glorious cross on infidel soil. But oh, my beloved, one mission would not be enough for me. I would want to preach the Gospel on all five continents simultaneously and even to the most remote isles."

One of the nuns who organizes the tours told a journalist: "It is not bones that people meet when they come to see the reliquary. They are meeting a friend." When her relics came to America, the *New York Times* called her the "Emily Dickinson of Roman Catholic sainthood."

CECILIA EUSEPI
(Italy, 1910–1928)

The youngest of eleven children on a small farm, she was sent to a convent school at age six. In her early teens she hoped to become a missionary with the Sisters of Mary, but she was weak from tuberculosis and was sent back to her village, confined to bed.

Her confessor urged her to keep a journal, and she wrote her autobiography in a school exercise book. She called it *The Story of a Clown.*

She wrote: "Sometimes in my amazement I wonder what Jesus ever saw in me that was so attractive as to draw Him to my nothingness." After all, she was devoted and prayed, but was otherwise unremarkable. She was, she wrote, "a half-stupid clown, good for nothing."

She died at eighteen. According to an elderly farmer who lived nearby, "When she died, some people said that a saint had died. But others claimed that she was just good, a good girl who had suffered, and they criticized these others for insisting on making a saint of her." In 2012 she was indeed made a saint.

EDVIGE CARBONI
(Italy, 1880–1952)

On the day she was born, her mother had a vision of a luminous host in a monstrance. A few days later, the baby developed a lump on her chest in the form of a cross. At five she took a vow of chastity, which she repeated daily for the rest of her life. Friends reported that, as a child, when she prayed her room would be filled with a blinding light, in which could be seen the figures of saints and angels.

To help her mother, who was ill, she left school after third grade. Sent out at night to buy food, her guardian angel would accompany her and wait outside the store, so she would not be afraid. At fifteen, she wanted to become a nun, but she had to care for her large family.

Nevertheless, Jesus chose her to be a victim soul, as St. John Bosco himself told her in a vision, "to repair for so many offenses that He constantly receives, especially because of immodest fashion, and for there to be peace among nations." The Virgin Mary told her, "My daughter, promise me to suffer all tribulation, rejection, scorn, and sufferings for the conversion of communists." St. John Bosco appeared again in 1941 and said: "My little daughter, remember that you have offered yourself as victim for the liberation of poor Russians from Bolshevism, sworn enemy to God. Pray so that soon the Crucified One can enter Russia."

An angel placed a crown of thorns on her head and for a few days she could not open her eyes. She received the transverberation: An angel wounded her heart, and one could see the skin over it blistered, radiating an intense heat; her night shirts had burn marks on them. She received the stigmata, but she asked Jesus to remove it so that she could continue working. She levitated while in prayer.

The devil tormented her. He scratched her, threw stones at her head, kicked her legs so hard she could barely walk, even took the gold fillings from her teeth. He broke dishes, mirrors, and windows, and scattered her flour, pasta, and polenta on the floor. He poured water on her bed (but the Virgin Mary herself dried it out). He undid her knitting. Once, she wrote, he "grabbed my bag and took the 100 liras that I had to go shopping. He took the money and turned it into ashes."

But her guardian angel helped her. Although she was barely literate, he dictated the letters she wrote, some of them in Latin. He made the beds when she was ill and cooked for her. One day, Jesus came to help with the laundry. She said he only pretended to wash the clothes, but had not touched them. He commanded it and the clothes became white and folded.

During the Second World War, the Virgin Mary came to her, weeping. She explained: "I am crying because I cannot appease the anger of my Son against the human race. If men don't do penance, the war will not end and much blood will be spilled. My daughter, immodest fashions and dishonesty have enraged God."

Soldiers who died in the war—one of them a Russian—came to her and asked her to pray for them. A teacher who was killed in a bombing told her that she only needed one more mass to be liberated from Purgatory. A priest who gave lectures at the University of Rome denying the real presence of Jesus in the Eucharist, and for whom she used to pray forgiveness, came to her after his death. He told her that he had been condemned because of the books he had written against the faith. To prove that this vision was not her imagination, he picked up a book in her room and it burst into flames.

In August 1941, Jesus took her to visit heaven. She wrote:

> I went walking up to a beautiful gate which had two angels, one on each side guarding it. The gate had a sign which read "Those who are dishonest and immodest cannot enter." The angels made me enter. I happily entered. It was a piece of Heaven. How beautiful! Plants and flowers I had never been seen before. The floor was covered with pearls and precious flowers. . . and everyone was singing happily.

During the war, when things were scarce, Jesus gave her some shoes and a skirt, St. John Bosco brought her half a kilo of rice, and St. Dominic Savio brought her coffee.

She had the gift of bilocation. She traveled with St. Sebastian to a town far away in Italy where a man was about to commit suicide. In another town, she persuaded a dying man to accept the last rites. During the war, she twice visited Cardinal Mindszenty in prison in Hungary. Jesus took her to visit Monsignor Cuthbert O'Gara, Passionist Bishop of Nanking, who had been imprisoned by the communists in China. As she hovered above them, out of reach, the guards screamed: "She is the witch of the Pope! She is a witch!"

She went to Moscow during the war and entered Stalin's room in the Kremlin. She said he had such an ugly stare that it made you afraid to look at him, and that he was shaking his fist, saying: "I am the strong and terrible enemy of God." She told him: "You have to convert. But if you want to be God's eternal enemy, you will be." But he responded: "I will never convert. I will be God's enemy forever."

She wrote in her diary:

While I was praying in front of the Crucifix, a person appeared to me suddenly all in flames, and I heard a voice say: "I am Benito Mussolini. The Lord has allowed me to come to you in order to get some relief from my sufferings in Purgatory. I beg you as an act of charity to offer for me all your prayers, sufferings, and humiliations for two years, if your director allows it. God's mercy is infinite but so is His justice. One cannot enter Heaven until one has paid the last penny of the debt owed to Divine Justice. Purgatory is terrible for me because I waited until the last moment to repent."

Some years later she wrote:

On a spring day in 1951, Jesus told me after Holy Communion: "This morning the soul of Benito Mussolini has entered into Heaven."

She died in 1952. In 1968, the process toward her beatification began with an investigation by the Diocese of Rome. In 1994, Pope John Paul II named her a Servant of God and the case was turned over to the Congregation for the Causes of Saints. They ruled *nihil obstat* ("nothing against"). In 2017, Pope Francis named her as Venerable, and in 2018 he approved a miracle attributed to the intercession of the Venerable Servant of God, Edvige Carboni, the final step before beatification.

III.

THE AFTERLIFE

OMNIPOTENSVIRTVSMAIESTASALTASABAOTH
EXCELSVSDOMINVSVIRTVTVMSVMMECREATOR
FORMATORMVNDIHOMINVMTVVEREREDEMPTOR
TVMEALAVSVIRTVGLORIACVNCTASALVSQVE
TVREXTVDOCTORTVESRECTORCAREMAGISTER
TVPASTORPASCENSPROTECTORVERVSOVILIS
PORTIOTVQEMEASANCTESALVATORETAVCTOR
DVXVIALVXVITAMERCESBONAIANVAREGNIES
VOXSENSVSVERBVMVIRTVTVMLAETAPROPAGO
ADTEDIREXITCVMVLANSNVNCDIRIGOVERBA
MENSMEATELOQVITVRMENTISINTENTIOTOTA
QVICQVIDLINGVAMANSORATETBVCCABEATE
CORHVMILEETVITAISTASACRATAVOLVNTAS
OMNIATELAVDANTETCANTANTCRISTESERENE
NAMQ:EGOTEDOMINVMPRONVSETIAETVSADORO
ATQECRVCIDEMISETVHINCDOSALVTANS
SPEMOROTERAMVSARAMARASVMARETOROHINC
HOCMEAMSTARDORCLARVSHOCIGNISAMORIS
HOCMEAMENSPOSCITPRIMVMHOCFAMENTORA
HOCSITISESTANIMIMANDENDIMAGNACVPIDO
VTMETVPIESVSCIPIABONECRISTEPERARAM
OBLATVMFAMVLVMQODVICTIMASIMTVAIESVS
HOSTIAQODTVASIMMEETCRVCIFIXIOTOTVM
IAMTVACONSVMATETPASSIOMITIGETAESTVM
CARNALEMVITIACONFRINGATDEPRIMETIRAM
REFRENETLINGVAMPITATISVERBAREPONAT
MENTEMPACIFICETVIAMDEDVCATHONESTAM
NAMQVETVVSQVANDOTOTOFVLGESCETOLYMPO
IGNEVSADVENTVSTORREBITTARDORINIQOS
TEMPESTASSTRIDETCORNVIAMMVGITETORBE
ANTEAPPAREBITQVANDOCRVCISAERESIGNVM
TVMROGOMEERIPIATFLAMMISVLTRICIB;IPSA
CVICANOLVRECANAMHVSVERSIBVSORE
CORDEMANVSEMPERDOSMEMORABILECANTV
QVODDEDERATVITAEMMENTERINARA
QANDOIPSAIESVSCLOABERVITIMO
INFERNIREQIEMNVNCARCEPOLORVM
DAMIHIHOCPOSCOSPEROEAOMNIACREDO
QVAEPROMISISTIHOCTENIATEFIDEQE
QVODVERAXFACISORDINEOMNIAVERO
INVNCADSVPEROSINCAELISRITETRIVMPHAS
OLAVSALMACRVCISSEMPERSINEFINEVALETO

THE AFTERLIFE

In the Glödnitz Valley of Carinthia they used to tell, until quite recently, the story of two sheep herders, old friends, who made a pact: When one died, he would come back to tell the other what he saw. Not long after, one of them indeed died and did indeed come back.

He said: "It's not what I thought it would be. It's not what you think it will be. They're very strict about the rules." Then he disappeared.

A GUIDE TO THE ILLUSTRATIONS

You could mistake the grid poems of Hrabanus Maurus's *In honorem sanctae crucis* for word searches. Searching them does not yield words, however, but layers of meaning, intended to exemplify the beauty and complexity of God's creation. *Carmina figurata* (figure poems), which form shapes with their words, trace their history back to the Hellenistic era. Hrabanus Maurus's early ninth-century collection is one of the high points of the form: a work of extraordinary intricacy and ambition. In it are 28 grids of letters that spell out poems, but also conceal phrases, and significant numbers, revealed by superimposed shapes and images.

Hrabanus Maurus (c. 780–856 CE), was a key figure in the Carolingian Renaissance. He was born in Mainz to a noble family, and offered as a *puer oblatus* to the Benedictine abbey of Fulda, as a child. He was ordained deacon there in 801 and elected abbot in 822. With him at the helm, Fulda became a center of book production and learning. He was elected Archbishop of Mainz in 847.

Hrabanus is sometimes known as "*Praeceptor Germaniae*" (the teacher of Germany). He wrote widely, producing works on grammar, mathematics, education, scriptural commentary, an encyclopaedia, countless homilies, hymns, and poetry. In *In honorem sanctae crucis*, written c. 810–14, mathematics and theology find mystical, poetic union. The work survives in eighty-one manuscripts, ranging in date from the early ninth to the sixteenth century. Four manuscripts survive that were copied at Fulda during the time of his abbacy.[1] It is likely, therefore, that these witnesses represent his vision for the work, and all subsequent copies are more or less faithful renderings of his original vision. The final image (p. 152) from a manuscript produced at Fulda, shows Hrabanus presenting his work to Pope Gregory IV.

The 28 poems of the collection mirror the 24 books of the Old Testament in the Hebrew tradition and the four Gospels. The first 24 poems meditate on a numerological theme (apart from poem 1 and poem 12) while the final four have no numerological significance. Poems 1 and

150

12 act as markers—they discuss Christ and Christ as the Second Adam. After Poem 12, we find a new thematic sequence. Poems 13 through 24 trace a narrative from the Nativity to the Apocalypse. Poem 24 meditates on the number 144, gesturing to a verse from Revelation (known as "Apocalypse" in the Middle Ages): "Then I looked, and behold, on Mount Zion stood the Lamb and with him 144,000 who had his name and his Father's name written on their foreheads" (14:1).

28 is a perfect number: the sum of all its divisors (1, 2, 4, 7, 14). Within the collection the poems are of different size, having a variable number of letters per line. The variation in size has been carefully constructed to reflect these very divisors. So, one of the poems has 41 letters per line, two of them have 36, four of them have 39, seven of them have 35, and fourteen of them have 37. Dear reader—stay with me—we have only just begun.

Such numerological complexity would evade the casual reader, or glancer, whose attention would likely be drawn to the shapes that overlay the poems. But the poems invite deeper examination, exhorting us to read ruminatively (from the Latin *ruminatio* meaning to "chew over"). The images that overlay the poems pull out key phrases. To aid the reader in comprehending the poems, Hrabanus included a commentary alongside each one. In the manuscripts produced at Fulda, the poem appears on the verso (the left-hand side of a double page spread) and the explanation on the next recto (i.e., the right-hand side of a double page spread). In keeping with a work in praise of the cross, all but one of the overlaid figures form a cruciform.[2]

In Poem 2 (p. 124) we see a cross inside a square. The overlaid colors on the cross and square highlight six hexameters, which each address the cross, opening with the invocation, "O crux…" Hrabanus's explanation instructs that these hexameters should be read in a particular order. The reader should not begin in the top left-hand corner of the grid, which is also the start of the poem, but instead begin at the top of the cross's shaft running down and then run left to right across the crossbeam.[3] In so doing, the reader makes the sign of the cross as they read, the poem inviting a sort of devout performance to understand its meaning.

Poem 7 contains four overlaid circles of different colors (p. 24). The

PONTIFICEM SUMMUM SALUATOR CHRISTE TUE RE

PRESUL EXIMIUS SIT RITE GREGORIUS ALMA

ET SALUUM NOBIS PASTORE MINSAECULA SERUA

ECLESIAE CUSTOS DOCTOR QUE FIDELIS IN AULA

poem is a kind of verse map of the world. The four circles represent the four continents, while the letters picked out in the circles refer to the cardinal directions (the winds), the four elements, the four seasons and the four temporal divisions. The circles read:

> *Ver, oriens, ignis, aurora hac parte relucent*
>   Spring, east, fire, sunrise gleam in this region
> *Autumus, zefirus, tellus, et vespera hic*
>   Autumn, west wind, earth and sunset are found here
> *Arcton, hiems, limpha, media nox ecce locatate*
>   Behold, north wind, winter, water and midnight are located here
> *Aer, aestas, auster, acri hic sit meridesque*
>   Air, summer, south wind and midday are here in the sky[4]

The overlaid shapes also capture numbers of letters with particular significance. Thus, Poem 7 captures 28 letters in its four circles (28 is, of course, the number of perfection). Poem 9 (p. 88), on the 365¼ days in the year, captures 365 letters in its overlaid shapes. It does this with four elongated hexagons, 19 lines down or 19 characters across, totaling 364 letters, with a single letter at the meeting point bringing the total to 365. The hexagonal shape reflects the six hours in its six angles, making 24 hours in the four hexagons. The hexagon also reflects the six hours of the ¼ day added up every leap year to form an extra day.

The final poem in the collection, Poem 28 (p. 148), contains a portrait of the author himself. At the center of the grid is a golden cross on which appears a palindromic acrostic:

> *ORO TE RAMUS ARAM ARA SUMAR ET ORO*
> I pray, O cross and altar, to be saved through you

(Hrabanus was fond of palindromes, which appear in the overlaid shapes of the preceding two poems in the collection.) In Poem 28, the letter "M" forms the central point of the cross, the hinge on which the phrase repeats itself vertically. Beneath the cross the author kneels. In some later manuscripts, like the one reproduced here, his eyes are lifted in supplication to the glittering cross above him. Yet, in the manuscripts copied during his abbacy, his gaze is directed into the field of letters, or back to the earlier poems in the collection, as if admiring his own numero-linguistic acrobatics.

Later ages have not looked so favorably on *In honorem sanctae crucis*, feeling that the poetry strains under the weight of its own artifice. H. Dümmler criticized Hrabanus's "torturous and ungainly meanderings."[5] In his *Poetry of the Carolingian Renaissance*, Peter Godman wrote of Hrabanus that "the satisfaction he describes finding in the act of writing is seldom shared by his readers."[6] Still, *In honorem sanctae crucis* is an act of devotion in words. And devotion often requires labor to reach enlightenment.

1. Vaticana, Biblioteca Apostolica Vaticana Reginensis Latinus 124; Paris BNF MS lat. 2423; Amiens Bibliothèque Municipale 223; Turin, Biblioteca Nazionale Universitaria K. II 20. See M. Perrin, *Rabani Mauri In honorem Sanctae Crucis* (Turnhout: Brepols, 1997), pp. xxx–xxxi.
2. The only exception is Poem 22, which forms a large Chi- Rho (the monogram of the first 2 Greek letters of ΧΡΙΣΤΟΣ *Christos*). This visually links the poems to an earlier cycle of *carmina figurata* by P. Optatianus Porfyrius, composed for the Emperor Constantine. On P. Optatianus Porfyrius, see William Schipper, "Hrabanus Maurus in Anglo-Saxon England", in *Early Medieval Studies in Memory of Patrick Wormald*, ed. by Stephen Baxter and others (Farnham: Ashgate, 2009), pp. 283–300 (p. 287).
3. In fact Hrabanus refers to the left as the right and vice versa, as the point of view is that of the cross looking out at the reader.
4. Translations from: David F. Bright, "Carolingian Hypertext: Visual and Textual Structures in Hrabanus Maurus, *In honorem Sanctae Crucis,*" in *Classics Renewed*:
5. Quoted in Bright, "Carolingian Hypertext," p. 355.
6. Peter Godman, *Poetry of the Carolingian Renaissance* (Norman: University of Oklahoma Press, 1985), p. 43.

THE ILLUSTRATIONS

Manuscript sources:

Amiens, Bibliothèque Municipale, MS 223, f. 2v
Made c. 825–50, at the abbey of Fulda.

Cambridge, Trinity College, MS B. 16.3
Made in the 10th century, origin unknown or disputed.

Bern, Burgerbibliothek, Cod. 9
Made at the beginning of 11th century, in central or southern France.

Paris, Bibliothèque Nationale De France MS lat. 11685
Made c. 1040–1060, in the Benedictine Abbey of Saint-Germain-des-Prés in Paris.

Munich, Bayerische Staatsbibliothek, clm. 8201
Made c. 1414/15, in Metten.

Page 1
Originally a blank leaf subsequently covered in short poems by Hrabanus Maurus, as well as biographical information relating to him. These 16th-century annotations were made by Jacques Du Breul (1528–1614), the claustral prior of the Benedictine Abbey of Saint-Germain-des-Prés in Paris. The following poem (A5) dedicated to Louis the Pious—son of Charlemagne—can be seen through the parchment.[1]
Paris, Bibliothèque Nationale De France MS lat. 11685, folio 5r

Page 2
Poem to Louis the Pious (A5), depicting Charlemagne's son as *miles Christi*. Not all manuscripts contain this poem and the other prefatory material. It has been argued that this poem was written later than the rest of the collection, to celebrate Louis's imperial restoration in 834.[2]
Paris, Bibliothèque Nationale De France MS lat. 11685, folio 5v

Page 10
Poem 4 (B4), depicting four angels. The top two are the fiery seraphim from Isaiah 6: 2–6. The two below are the cherubim—the celestial guardians of the Ark of the Covenant. The poem meditates on the number 6—the seraphim have six wings. In *De Universo*, Hrabanus notes that these six wings mirror the six days that it took God to create the heavens and Earth.[3] 37 characters per line; part of the "Christ-sequence" (Poems 2–11).
Cambridge, Trinity College, MS B. 16.3, folio 6v

Page 17
Poem 5 (B5), depicting four squares around a cross. Meditates on the cross and

the house of God. The cross contains an inscription repeated top to bottom and left to right: "*INCLYTA CRUX DOMINI CHRISTI FUNDAMEN ET AVLAE*" (The glorious Cross of Our Lord it is the foundation of Christ's church). "*Christi*" is written as the Greek *chi* and *rho* (XP)—the first two letters of the Greek word ΧΡΙΣΤΟΣ (*Christos*). In this way, the X forms the center point of the cross. The inscriptions in the four squares relate to the patriarchs (bottom left), prophets (bottom right), apostles (top left) and martyrs (top right), to be read in this order, such that the martyrs are the last and most significant. 35 characters per line; part of the "Christ-sequence" (Poems 2–11).
Munich, Bayerische Staatsbibliothek, clm. 8201, f. 45v

Page 24
Poem 7 (B7), depicting four circles. Meditation on the "tetrads of the world," i.e., the four continents, the cardinal directions (the winds), the four elements, the four seasons and the four temporal divisions. 144 letters are highlighted. 144 is a number of significance (see discussion of Poem 24 above). The poem focuses on the number 4 (36 x 4). 35 characters per line; part of the "Christ-sequence" (Poems 2–11).
Bern, Burgerbibliothek, Cod. 9, folio 3v

Page 33
Poem 8 (B8), depicting a branched cross, with twelve points. Meditates on the numerological significance of the number 12, which is important as there are twelve months, twelve signs of the zodiac, twelve winds, twelve tribes of Israel, twelve gates to the New Jerusalem, and twelve apostles. 37 characters per line; part of the "Christ-sequence" (Poems 2–11).
Cambridge, Trinity College, MS B. 16.3, folio 10v

Page 40
Poem 14 (B14), depicting Greek or Roman numerals, arranged in a cruciform. Meditation on time: from the Creation to the Passion, and the number 5,231 (a prime number). At the center of the cruciform is Γ (gamma), in a coral color (= 3 in the system of Greek numerals); beyond this are 4 Z (zetas) in brown (=7), then 4 T (taus) (=300) and finally 4 ∞ in yellow. This symbol does not designate infinity, as it was not used as such until the 17th century, but is one of the Roman numerals for 1,000 (originally CIↃ, also CↃ). Thus (1000 x 4) + (300 x 4) + (7 x 4) + 3 = 5,231. The inscription starting at the top ∞ reads, "*EN CRUCIS HAEC SPECIES CONPUTAT HANC NUMERUM IESUS QUO EST PASSUS IN ARVIS BENE MONSTRAT HONOREM*" (Behold, this figure of the cross computes that number [which] well shows the honor by which Jesus suffered in the fields). 39 characters per line; part of the "Adam-sequence" (Poems 13–24).
Bern, Burgerbibliothek, Cod. 9, folio 10v

Page 49
Poem 18 (B18), depicting letters of different colors forming four triangles and arranged in a cross-shape. Meditates on the numerological significance of the number 40. Forty is a number of significance because Christ fasted for forty days in the desert before his temptation. Forty days was also the period of time between Christ's Resurrection and Ascension. Each triangle is composed of ten letters. The first row of letters in the uppermost triangle reads "Crux," and the inscription "*CRUX SACRA, TU AETERNI ES REGIS VICTORIA CHRISTI*" (Sacred Cross, you are eternal victory of Christ the King) should be read top to bottom, left to right. 37 characters per line; part of the "Adam-sequence" (Poems 13–24). Bern, Burgerbibliothek, Cod. 9, folio 14v

Page 59
Poem 19 (B19), depicting five Xs arranged in a cruciform. Meditates on the numerological significance of the number 50. After the central letter in each X is counted twice, as the letters are counted first through one line and then another (as if the counter is forming a cross), there are ten letters picked out in each X, bringing the total number of letters picked out to fifty. Similarly, the inscription must be read in the same way, beginning with the top left-hand corner of the X, moving to the bottom right, and then the top right to bottom left. For the inscription to make sense, the central letter of each X must be repeated. 37 characters per line; part of the "Adam-sequence" (Poems 13–24). Cambridge, Trinity College, MS B. 16. 3, folio 21v

Page 68
Poem 13 (B13), depicting four crosses in a cruciform. The theme of the poem is the Temple, which took 46 years to build, but only three days to restore, but also Christ in the Virgin's womb for 276 days (i.e., nine months, six days). There are 276 letters in the four crosses. Hrabanus, following Augustine's *De Trinitate*, notes that the 46 years it took to build the Temple multiplied by 6 makes 276. Dividing 276 by the four ends of the cross gives us 69. Six and nine are important as the nine months and six days of the Virgin's pregnancy, as well as the sixth day of Creation when man was created along with the nine orders of angels. 35 characters per line; part of the "Adam-sequence" (Poems 13–24). Cambridge, Trinity College, MS B. 16. 3, folio 15v

Page 79
Poem 25 (B25), on "Amen" and "Alleluia." The word "Alleluia" can be made out by starting at the top and moving downward, then moving left to right, as if making the sign of the cross. The word "Amen" appears in a cross on the poem's center point. Again, the word can be made out by tracing the letters in making a cross. 37 characters per line. Bern, Burgerbibliothek, Cod. 9, folio 21v

Page 88
Poem 9 (B9), depicting four converging hexagons. Meditates on the 365¼ days in the year, captures 365 letters in its overlaid shapes. The hexagons contain 364 letters, with a single letter at the meeting point bringing the total to 365. The hexagonal shape reflects the six hours in its six angles, making twenty-four hours in the four hexagons. The hexagon also reflects the six hours of the quarter day added up every leap year to form an extra day. 41 characters per line; part of the "Christ-sequence" (Poems 2–11).
Paris, Bibliothèque Nationale De France MS lat. 11685, folio 16v

Page 99
Poem 11 (B11), depicting five squares. Meditates on the five books of Mosaic Law, i.e. the first five books of the Bible known as the Pentateuch: Genesis, Exodus, Leviticus, Numbers, and Deuteronomy. The names of each book can be found in each of the five squares. 36 characters per line; part of the "Christ-sequence" (Poems 2–11).
Cambridge, Trinity College, MS B. 16.3, folio 13v

Page 109
Poem 15 (B15), on the Evangelists and the Lamb of God. The images show the symbols of the Evangelists (the authors of the Gospels). John appears at the top as an eagle, the lamb in the middle, Mark as a winged lion on the left, and Luke as a winged ox on the right. Focuses on the number 4 (for the four Gospels). On the lamb, the words "*ecce angus dei*" (behold the lamb of God) can be seen. On the rectangles under each evangelist symbol are quotations from the opening verses of each of the Gospels, e.g. John: "*In principio erat v*[…]" (In the beginning was the w[…]). 36 characters per line; part of the "Adam-sequence" (Poems 13–24).
Cambridge, Trinity College, MS B. 16.3, folio 17v

Page 117
Poem 17 (B17), depicting eight octagons. Meditates on the eight Beatitudes (as drawn from Matthew 5: 3–12). Each octagon represents a different Beatitude. Here, readers are invited to begin symbolically at the base of the cross, where the bottom octagon refers to the blessed poor of Christ ("*REGNA POLI DOMINUS VULT PAUPERIS ESSE BEATI*"). After the second octagon up from the bottom, readers must proceed to the left-hand side of cruciform and read each octagon in a horizontal sequence. Arranging the Beatitudes in this way means that the octagon referring to the blessed martyrs appears at the top of the cross (see note to page 17). 39 characters per line; part of the "Adam-sequence" (Poems 13–24).
Cambridge, Trinity College, MS B. 16.3, folio 19v

Page 124
Poem 2 (B2), depicting a cross and colored margins. The overlaid colors on the cross and square highlight six hexameters, which each address the cross, opening with the invocation, "*O crux…*" Hrabanus's explanation instructs that these hexameters should be read in a particular order. The reader should not begin in the top left-hand corner of the grid, which is also the start of the poem, but instead begin at the top of the cross's shaft and then continue left to right across the crossbeam. 35 characters per line; part of the "Christ-sequence" (Poems 2–12).
Cambridge, Trinity College, MS B. 16.3, folio 4v

Page 139
Poem 20 (B20), depicting four lambdas. In the system of Greek numerals, lambda (λ) has a value of 30. The poem meditates on the numerological significance of the number 120 (i.e., 30 x 4). 37 characters per line; part of the "Adam-sequence" (Poems 13–24).
Cambridge, Trinity College, MS B. 16.3, folio 22v

Page 148
Poem 28 (B28), depicting a portrait of the author himself, beneath a cross. The cross contains a palindromic acrostic, "*ORO TE RAMUS ARAM ARA SUMAR ET ORO*" (I pray, O cross and altar, to be saved through you). 35 and 43 letters per line. The final poem of the collection.
Cambridge, Trinity College, MS B. 16.3, folio 30v

Page 152
Hrabanus presents his work to Pope Gregory IV.
Amiens, Bibliothèque Municipale, MS 223, folio 2v

Descriptions of each poem are indebted to David F. Bright, "Carolingian Hypertext: Visual and Textual Structures in Hrabanus Maurus, *In honorem Sanctae Crucis,*" in *Classics Renewed: Reception and Innovation in the Latin poetry of Late Antiquity*, ed. by Scott McGill and Joseph Pucci (Heidelberg: Universitätsverlag, Winter, 2016), pp. 355–84 (p. 381).
1. (A–) or (B–) refers to the names of the poems in: M. Perrin, *Rabani Mauri In honorem Sanctae Crucis* (Turnhout: Brepols, 1997). In Perrin's scheme, (B–) distinguishes the poems from the prefatory material (A–) and Hrabanus's explanations (C–), which appear on the facing page.
2. "Louis the Pious as Miles Christi: The Dedicatory Image in Hrabanus Maurus's *De Laudibus Sanctae Crucis*" in *Charlemagne's Heir: New Perspectives on the Reign of Louis the Pious (814–840)*, ed. by P. Godman and R. Collins (Oxford: Oxford University Press, 1990), pp. 605–28.
3. Yves Christie, "The Apocalypse in the Monumental Art of the Eleventh through Thirteen Centuries," in *The Apocalypse in the Middle Ages*, ed. by Richard Kenneth Emmerson, Bernard McGinn (Ithaca: Cornell University Press, 1992), pp. 234–59 (p. 254).

Eliot Weinberger's books of literary essays include *Karmic Traces, An Elemental Thing*, and *The Ghosts of Birds*. His political writings are collected in *What I Heard About Iraq* and *What Happened Here: Bush Chronicles*. The author of a study of Chinese poetry translation, *19 Ways of Looking at Wang Wei*, he is a translator of the poetry of Bei Dao, the editor of *The New Directions Anthology of Classical Chinese Poetry*, and the general editor of the series *Calligrams: Writings from and on China*. He was formerly the literary editor of the Murty Classical Library of India. Among his many translations of Latin American poetry and prose are *The Poems of Octavio Paz*, Paz's *In Light of India*, Vicente Huidobro's *Altazor*, Xavier Villaurrutia's *Nostalgia for Death*, and Jorge Luis Borges' *Seven Nights* and *Selected Non-Fictions*. His work has been translated into over thirty languages, and appears frequently in the *London Review of Books*. He was born in New York City, where he still lives, and has been publishing with New Directions since 1975.

Dr. Mary Wellesley is a Research Affiliate at the British Library whose research focuses on medieval manuscripts. She writes and reviews widely, her work regularly appearing in the *London Review of Books, Daily Telegraph, Times Literary Supplement*, among other publications. Her book, *Hidden Hands: Manuscripts That Made Us* will be published by Quercus in the United Kingdom and Basic Books in the U.S.